Moving to
Main Street, U.S.A.

How We Left Our Home, Took the Kids, and Moved to the Doorstep of Walt Disney World

Michele Atwood

Theme Park Press
www.ThemeParkPress.com

Editor: Bob McLain
Layout: Artisanal Text

ISBN 978-1-68390-052-8
Printed in the United States of America

Theme Park Press | www.ThemeParkPress.com
Address queries to bob@themeparkpress.com

Contents

1   Once Upon a Time 1

2   Real Life vs Dreaming 7

3   Virtual Reality? 11

4   I've Got a Dream 15

5   Moving Forward 19

6   See Ya Real Soon 25

7   A Whole New World 27

8   Now What? 33

9   Disney from a Different Perspective 35

10 Adjusting 39

11 Meet-up Time and More Adjusting 45

12 Making the Most of Summer 49

13 Here Comes Reality 53

14 Fall and Family 59

15 Expanding Our Horizons 65

16 Meeting Our Disney Ohana 67

17 Christmas Cheer 71

18 Wrapping Things Up and Going Home .. 75

19 Let's Do This 81

20 Another First 85

21 Family First 89

22 Spring Has Sprung 93

23 On the Scene 97

24 Feet on Ground, Head Elsewhere 101

25 We Made It 105

26 The Adventure Continues 109

27 Food, Wine, and Finding Time 113

28 Celebrate Good Times (on a Budget) 117

29 Tis the Season 121

30 Ups and Downs 125

31 Expect the Unexpected 129

32 Finding Strength 133

33 Living the Dream the Best We Can 137

About the Author 141

More Books from Theme Park Press 143

CHAPTER ONE

Once Upon a Time

Once upon a time ... in a suburb just south of Detroit, Michigan, my Disney obsession began.

Being the daughter of a school teacher, my mom wanted to instill reading and such in me from the get-go, and one of the first books I remember her buying me was Disney's *Sleeping Beauty*. Sure, I had the Dr. Seuss collection, but the Disney ones always stuck out more. I remember when I was around 4 or 5, my parents took me to my first movie in a theater, and it was a re-release of *Lady and the Tramp*. Yes, more Disney. I had no idea why I loved it so much, or what else the world of Disney had to offer, but by the time I was 6, I was able to find out.

My dad always had this philosophy of not taking kids on vacation until they were at least 5, for two reasons: one, because when kids are a little older, they are easier to control, and two, because he felt a child won't remember their trip if they're too young. Good reasons.

When they finally took me on a big vacation, of course it was to Walt Disney World. At the time, it was just the Magic Kingdom, and I don't remember a whole lot about it, but I sure do remember Cinderella Castle. I remember riding "it's a small world" and Mr. Toad's Wild Ride. Mostly, I recall the feeling of absolute bliss, and I loved it. Disney was so much more than the books I had in my bedroom or the movies we watched. It's a passion deep within, and once it starts, it's near impossible to shake.

Most of our family vacations were "up north," as we call it in Michigan, meaning we drove a few hours north of where we lived to spend a week on a lake in a cottage. I have great memories of those trips, too, but I couldn't stop thinking, 'I really want to go back to Disney World.'

Fast forward a few years to high school. It's a rite of passage: once a person makes it to the 12th grade, they take their big senior trip with their friends. My parents were pretty strict, and I wasn't sure of being able to do what my friends were doing. The school put together a Caribbean cruise for the senior trip, and many were going, but not me. Not because I couldn't; I didn't even ask to go. Instead, I had hatched a plan that I was going to Disney World that year for spring break. Sure, people thought I was nuts, not wanting to go on a cruise with friends, unattended for the first time, but I had no interest.

That year for my birthday I asked for money instead of gifts, then set aside a piggy bank and wrote "Florida Fund" on it, because I was going to find a way to get back to Disney. After some finagling, I ended up going to Disney World with a friend and a set of parents, instead of the usual wild spring break, but that's how I wanted it. Seeing the Magic Kingdom as a bigger "kid" put a whole new spin on it. I was 18 years old, I went on every ride, I saw the shows, took a ton of photos, and took it all in. I was in heaven.

When I went back to school once the week was over, everyone was talking about the wild time they had, whooping it up and partying, and then there was me, in my Disney World t-shirt talking about the most magical place I had ever been to. What's funny is no one made fun of that. Actually, they wanted to know about my trip, what we did, what Disney has to offer. I found that I quite liked talking Disney and giving advice on the subject. Little did I know that would come in handy years later.

The following year, it was summer vacation time, and there I was, bugging my parents to take us to Disney World. My brother is 9 years younger than me, and I knew he would love going there as well. I got my way, saved money for souvenirs and such, and we did plan a Florida vacation. The real destination was Sanibel Island, but I talked my mom and dad into staying the weekend near Disney World before we headed to the beach. Disney was so different then. I look back at photos from that trip and it's amazing how much has changed. There were trees up and down Main Street, and vines growing up the castle. There were fewer parades and no FastPasses at all. Let me touch on that one....

July in Florida is not only hot, but extremely busy at Disney World. My father has no patience for long lines, or heat, so he wasn't a happy camper on that trip. He did it for my brother and me; it certainly wasn't something he enjoyed. I believe we waited almost 2 hours to ride Space Mountain, and he was just done. I mean, done. From that trip on, he called Disney the "mouse park" and had no interest in going back. I felt the complete opposite. I still loved it, I didn't care that it was hot and crowded. It was my happy place; long lines and hot sun weren't going to stop me from wanting to go back, and it didn't.

When I started college, I planned to become a teacher like my mom. School was expensive, and so were the other things I wanted to do at that point in my life, so I ended up getting a full-time job in finance. I knew nothing about the stock market, but I was willing to learn, because hey, that's Disney money! I continued to go to school, and squeezed in Disney trips when I could afford them. I lived at home with my parents until I married my high school sweetheart when I was 24 (and yes, it's a no-brainer, we spent our honeymoon at Disney World).

I was living on my own, and could have chosen any place to vacation at, but it was always Disney. Going to Disney for the first time on my own was awesome. I didn't have to worry about doing what others wanted to do, didn't have to go turn in for the night at the hotel because others were tired; it was liberating. I loved it.

The year after the wedding, I planned another Disney trip. Two years after that, I had the idea that I was going to get my best friend and her husband to take a couples trip to Disney with us because they had never been there. This was my chance to use my Disney knowledge to show them a good time. We did indeed have fun, and it was great to be able to plan out an itinerary for the week to make sure I showed them the best of what Disney had to offer. We went to the parks, restaurants, Downtown Disney, Typhoon Lagoon.... We squeezed a lot into the 5 days that we were there.

All the years of visiting Disney, I never got to fully experience the now-closed Pleasure Island. Being at Disney with my best girlfriend was the perfect opportunity to hit the clubs at Disney, dance, and have more of that "liberating" fun. I miss Pleasure Island. Remember Mannequins, with the revolving dance floor? Ah, memories. People would ask me if I got tired of going to Disney World every year, and the answer was always no. I told people when it came to all things Disney, either you get it or you don't. I totally got it. My husband got it, he was right there with me, but as for my family and most friends, I think they thought I was a bit crazy, but I didn't mind.

The fall after the Disney trip we took with our friends, things changed in my life. I had been married for two years, was enjoying my freedom (from my parents, at least), and I was trying to figure out what I wanted to do with my life. I ended up staying in finance instead of going into teaching, and worked for one of the larger investment firms. It wasn't what I truly wanted to do, but it was something I fell into and the opportunity to work for a good company was there.

That summer I was also doing promotional work for a modeling company, and was going to work the auto-show circuit as a spokes-model for Chrysler. I was excited and scared at the same time. I didn't know if I should quit my finance job to travel for Chrysler, or if I should stay put at my secure job, even though it wasn't my ideal place to be. During this time, I found out I was pregnant with my first son. It was scary. I was in denial at first; I even took the pregnancy test over to my mom's house for a second opinion. I know, that's terrible, but I needed to be sure.

So yes, I was having a baby, and yes, I turned down the promotional jobs and stayed at my desk job during my pregnancy. My cousin worked with me, so it was nice to have someone to lean on daily at the office, especially since I was pretty sick that first trimester. Those nine months seemed to last an eternity, and I worked right up to the week I had my son, Andrew. My parents were excited to be getting a grandchild, and I knew my entire world was about to change. It changed for the better, and he was a handsome and happy baby. My company offered decent maternity leave, so I was home with Andrew, getting used to being a new mom and enjoying my time.

Once all the fuss settled down and I was in a routine, I started to think of one of the things I've always wanted to do ... take my own child to Disney World. Now, if I went my my dad's 5 year plan, then I had plenty of time to research a trip and save money. But everyone who knows me knew I wasn't going to wait until Andrew was almost school age. No way. Andrew was such a good baby, I could take him anywhere and he wasn't fussy, I knew he'd be fine to take to Disney. The planning soon began, and I was determined to take my new little man to my happy place.

Planning Disney trips was my thing. I loved doing the research, looking up photos online, and finding the best deals. Before I knew it, there was a plan in place, and I was taking my new baby to Disney. He was 11 months old. My parents asked me if I was "sure" I wanted to do that, being that he wouldn't remember the trip, but I knew it's what I wanted. I couldn't wait to get there.

We stayed at our usual spot, the Best Western Lake Buena Vista in the Downtown Disney area, and I was so excited. Taking Andrew to the Magic Kingdom for the first time, seeing his face when he met Mickey Mouse ... pure Disney magic. My heart was full.

Honestly, I learned quite a lot on that vacation. Going to Disney with a child is a whole different ballgame, and you have to be prepared and take so much more with you. I wasn't this carefree Disney-goer anymore. Now I had to have a diaper bag with bottles, wipes, baby clothes, just to name a few things. Getting through the parks with a stroller was fun the first time, too. I say that with the utmost sarcasm. Well, I shouldn't say it negatively, it was a learning experience, but after that week I was a pro. Also, I had no idea before, but you can take a baby on a lot of the rides at Disney. If the child can sit on your lap, they can go with you on smaller rides; no coasters, of course. That was pretty great, because we didn't have to use the baby swap option. We stayed together as a family, and it was an amazing week. There is something about seeing Disney through the eyes of your own children. It's hard to explain, but I know it's a feeling I won't ever forget. I'm so glad I didn't wait.

The following year, we planned another Disney trip, and my son was just short of two years old. Going to Disney with a toddler is also a learning experience. It was easy when he wasn't walking yet; I could just carry him or put him in the stroller. When we was two, he wanted to get down and walk. My mom flew down to Orlando to spend the second half of our trip with us so she could be with her first grandchild at the parks, too. Just like with the first time around, seeing Andrew interact with characters and go on the various attractions was a treat. I'll never forget, though, the first time I took him to see Wishes at the Magic Kingdom. We picked him up so he could see the show better, and it was pure magic. I could see the reflection of the fireworks in his eyes. The look of wonder and excitement on his little face is burned into my memory. I stood there and had tears running down my cheeks. Being there with him, seeing the magic continue though my own son, it was everything I hoped it would be, and more.

I never went back to work at the financial firm on a full-time basis, becoming instead a (mostly) stay-at-home mom. After that second

Disney trip with Andrew, I had some health issues, so I was glad that I could be home with him and not have to worry about being in an office. Being a stay-at-home mom was something I never envisioned for myself, but once I was put in that position, I enjoyed it. Plus, I was grooming my son for the Disney life, with Disney movies, story books, etc.

At the end of that summer, I found out that my second son was on the way. To help Andrew get excited for his little brother, we moved him out of the nursery and into a "big boy room" that was, you guessed it, decorated in full Disney theming. I went to Home Depot and got paint swatches from their Disney line, and ended up painting his new room in blue, red, and yellow, with Mickey heads on the ceiling. It was great, he loved it, so did I. Everything seemed to be falling into place. Life was pretty good.

The health issues I had prior to getting pregnant with my second son, Aidan, stuck around, and both he and I got very sick when I had him. I almost didn't make it, and it really changed me. We both got physically stronger, and were doing much better by the time we left the hospital. I felt very bonded to Aidan, because of what we went through; it was hard. I had a rough time with postpartum depression, but I didn't realize that's what it was, so of course I felt I could beat the blues by planning a trip to Disney with both boys.

Aidan, like Andrew, also went to Disney for the first time when he was 11 months old. Having a one year old and a 4 year old at Disney was something I thought would be challenging, but it was a great trip. I probably went overboard with taking photos, but seeing both my babies at my happy place was just what I needed at the time. Aidan had the same look of excitement and curiosity that Andrew had. He loved seeing the characters, he wasn't afraid of anything; we even took them to the water park. It was a good thing, all of it. My health was a bit shaky, but it didn't matter that week. Sometimes, it's just what the doctor ordered—or likely didn't order. I'll cherish that time with them. always.

CHAPTER TWO

Real Life vs Dreaming

As we all know, life isn't really a fairytale and things happen and take a turn for the worse, and that's exactly what happened. Within a year after that trip, I found myself divorced, living alone, raising two small boys, and with no job because I was a stay-at-home mom. My dreams of taking the boys to Disney the following year came to a screeching halt, and I had to do what I needed to do for the sake of my kids.

The economy in Michigan then was rough, but I knew I had to find something to help make ends meet. Finance was my background, but it took me months to find a job in that field, so I tried my hand at waitressing for the first time in my life, for about 9 months. I had no experience in being a server, but the managers at the Mexican restaurant where I applied gave me a shot, and I was grateful. When push comes to shove, and you have little mouths to feed, you do whatever you have to do. It was a humbling experience, but also kind of fun. I don't regret doing it.

I did end up getting another finance job in downtown Detroit, full time, and my babies had to go to daycare. Finance wasn't my passion, but again, it's a job and pays the bills, so I was thankful. There were days that I'd be sitting in my cubicle, looking across the Detroit river to Canada, daydreaming of being someplace else. I'd think to myself, I'm wasting time here, when I could be doing something else that I love, something that would allow me to spend more time with the kids. I had no idea what would happen, I was just praying that some answers would come. Things were hard, but I had hope that there was a silver lining somewhere. I wanted my happy ending, but I assumed it would have to wait. In the meantime, the only Disney fix I got was helping other people in my office plan their trips. I didn't mind helping others, even if I couldn't get to my happy place myself.

I always tell people that life is funny, and we never know what's going to happen, good or bad. The boys and I got lucky, and I reconnected with someone I knew from high school, my current husband, Scott. He accepted me, my sons, and everything else that came with the package, and after what seemed like a whirlwind, we were planning a wedding. I missed the family life, I wanted my boys to have that again, and thank God, we were getting just that.

When it came time to plan another wedding, it had been so long since I'd done anything like that, the only thing I knew for sure is that Disney needed to be a part of it. Scott was not a Disney fan, and I was intent on changing that. We had Cinderella-themed invitations and a cake topper, and we took a short honeymoon to Disney World. I needed to make a believer out of him. After a few days, he was beginning to understand why I loved Disney so much, and I was relieved. We were standing near Test Track in Epcot, and had an interesting conversation. Scott worked for a computer company in Detroit, and had an extensive background in code and technology. We were tossing around the idea of maybe creating a place online for people to share Disney vacation photos and stories—a community for Disney fans. Is that a crazy idea? Maybe. We'll talk more about that later.

The following year, my drive for family Disney trips returned with a vengeance and we took the kids back there, finally, after a hiatus. They were a little older, and really excited to go, since they didn't remember much from their previous trips. I had it all planned out, of course: we were going to stay at Pop Century Resort, try to visit all four parks, and have as good of a time as we could on a budget. We got lucky, because Disney contacted us, and since our trip was paid in full, they offered us an upgrade to Old Key West Resort and threw in free dining. I wanted to know what the catch was! No catch, they were trying to move people up from the value resorts so that they could sell more trips. I guess crowds were low. It worked out to our benefit and we had a fantastic trip that didn't cost us anything extra. Actually, we saved money with the free dining, and the kids got to do more character dinners than we planned.

On that trip, Scott and I started talking again about that Disney website idea. MySpace was on its way out, and Facebook was all the rage. We tossed around the idea of creating a Facebook type of site, but geared for Disney fans. I didn't know what that would entail, but I was willing to continue the conversation once we got home.

After we were home and the Disney magic started to wear off, I was missing it already. I always did once we had to get back to reality. So, we tried to put a plan in motion, and Scott began doing the coding to build this Disney site that we talked about. It took a long time to build, many months. Once the platform was built, it kind of sat there for a while, because I wasn't sure what to do with it. I loved to write, as well as loved to be a social butterfly, but I was working full time, raising two sons, and didn't have a ton of time to devote to our new project.

Remember how I said earlier that life is funny and changes when we least expect it? Well, that's an ongoing theme in my life. Again, the economy in Michigan was rough, and the financial firm I worked for was getting bought out. One of the owners had passed away, and the other founder was getting ready to retire. I worked in Detroit for almost 4 years, but I wasn't happy there. It was a job, but I wondered if I could do more. Granted, I didn't want to lose my job, I was scared, but that's exactly what happened. When I left my office at the Renaissance Center that day, I cried in the elevator. All the way down 21 floors, tears like a baby. What was I going to do now? Would my husband be upset? How were we going to make ends meet on one income? So many thoughts were running through my head. It was the longest elevator ride of my life. The crazy part is … by the time I got to my car and left the parking garage, my tears had stopped, and I actually felt relief. Relief. I had no clue why, but a weight had lifted off my shoulders.

I got home, Scott was not the least bit upset, he said we'd make it somehow, and we did. It wasn't easy, that's for sure, but as before, when life deals you a bad hand, you just push though it. In the four years I had my job in Detroit, I was lucky enough to have good insurance. I had some health issues and needed a few surgeries, and thank God, that was covered. So finance wasn't my dream, it never was, but it served a purpose and now it was time to figure out what to do next. I always felt like there was something else I could or should be doing, and it was time to explore that a bit more.

Going from working full time to being home again was an adjustment, but a good one. I hated having to send my boys to daycare, or make arrangements for them after school, and now I didn't have to. My younger son, Aidan, has issues with asthma; he's had them since he was about 8 months old. I used to have to call into work when he would get sick in the winter time, and now again, that wasn't an issue. No daycare costs, no work clothes to buy, no extra lunches ... maybe we could make something work.

After a few weeks of being home, the newness wore off and I started to get restless. I didn't want to be stuck in a cubicle anymore, and that was a relief, but I needed to find something else to fill the hours when the kids were at school and I had time to myself. When you're used to being busy, that alone time can be lonely. I began to get antsy. That Disney site I told you about earlier was still there ... just waiting. What do I do with this? Do I try to fill some of my down time with a little Disney magic? Sure, why not. That's exactly what I did. The platform was there, I just had to find a way reach out to other Disney fans and see if there was a want or a need for what we had built.

Facebook was something I hadn't really put much stock into, or time rather, because I hadn't had much opportunity to do so. I decided to get on there and get social with other Disney fans, once I figured out how to do that. Like with everything, it's trial and error. Once I started meeting others with the same interests as me, I thought the smart thing to do would be to create a Facebook page for our new Disney fan site, The Main Street Mouse (TMSM). At that point, we had nothing to lose. If people didn't like what we had to offer, I figured we'd find that out soon enough. I was also doing some Disney crafting in between, so Disney was already becoming my new "business," so to speak.

By the summertime, we actually began to get a following. Basically, all I was doing was writing about my favorite subject, and talking with others during the day, and boom! Disney friendships were being formed, and The Main Street Mouse began to take on a life of its own.

I thought we needed to give our readers more, even though I wasn't making a dime off of what I was doing. We started making TMSM charter member buttons and laminated member cards, and would send them out when someone new joined the site. This worked well at first, but so many people were joining, it got expensive and we couldn't keep up. We also created a chat room on the site where folks could talk Disney with others, and I set that up around the same time every night that summer. After the boys went to bed, of course. Those chats were so much fun. People got to know each other, and friendships were born. Actually, three of the people in those chat rooms still are with me today, but they are on staff now. It's crazy. Speaking of crazy....

CHAPTER THREE

Virtual Reality?

I was naïve to think that everyone in the virtual world was true blue and meant well. We met some great people, but we met some crazies, too. When I was growing up, I always took people at face value, and would believe someone until they gave me reason not to. Within months, I had been cyberstalked by a married man who was preying upon gals in the Disney community, met a person pretending to be a Disney cast member to get in good with us and write for the site, and learned that other Disney sites had started gunning for us. Why? I had no clue. Either we were doing something wrong, or doing something very right.

After all the online drama, we decided to take a time out, and pulled The Main Street Mouse offline. Yes, after all of that start-up effort, we were buried in extra work, soap opera-like drama, and it was costing us money. The online Disney community is rough, believe it or not, and I wasn't sure if I was cut out for it. What in the world did I get myself into? My hobby turned into a all-consuming hot mess and I had had enough. I kept TMSM's Facebook page active, sharing funny pictures and Disney news here and there, but the site itself was down. The hits were huge and crashing our server. With everything going on, we had gotten in over our heads. I still had my Disney fix with online friends through social media, and I began making more Disney crafts to fill the extra void.

In 2011, we finally made it back down to Walt Disney World for a family trip. We hadn't been there in two years; with my job being downsized, we just couldn't afford it. That trip was wonderful. We were able to take advantage of Disney's free dining offer, and stayed long enough to enjoy two resorts. I think we were gone 10 days, total. We did so much on that trip because I didn't know when we'd be able to return. Disney was our vacation of choice, always, so we needed to make the most of our time. Living 18 hours away from Disney was hard for us; it's where we wanted to be, but time and money got in the way.

The only "touring plan" I insisted on was making sure we visited the Magic Kingdom on the last full day of our trip. I love all the parks, but Magic Kingdom has my heart. We'd always stay until after the fireworks; Wishes was a major must-do. After the show, I'd stroll through the Emporium on Main Street to grab those last-minute souvenirs and take one more look around. One thing about our Disney vacations, I never took them for granted. I'd try to be in the moment, and take mental pictures of my family and surroundings, because I knew that in the blink of an eye, those moments would become memories. On that last night, before leaving the park, we'd always stop and take one more look at Cinderella Castle, and I'd cry. Now, that may sound crazy to some, but die-hard Disney fans get it. It's like our second home, and we miss it when we're not there.

As predicted, that trip to Disney World flew by, and it was time to get back to reality. We hit some more bumps in the road, but in my spare time, I still kept up with The Main Street Mouse online and still kept in touch with our former members. The Facebook page kept growing, and I started to get more requests to bring the site back. People missed it. Scott and I had many long conversations about it. Did we want to jump back into the fray of running our own site again? I wanted to give it another shot, but he was reluctant. He was still working long hours downtown, and he didn't see how much interaction we were still getting on social media. Not to mention, it was going to take a lot of time for him to build the site again; he was the one who did all the back-end coding, not me. This was just my hobby, and I never expected to turn things into a "real" job, but I missed it too.

After months of me doing some convincing, and Scott doing some coding, we finally had the new site almost built. The Main Street Mouse needed to be different this time. We didn't want it to just be a place for chats and games, we wanted more. This is where the blog came into play. As I said, Scott was working and I'd be the one to run things, so I had to be ready to write and keep people interested. Heck, I had already been talking to our readers almost daily, I felt I could meet the challenge.

We started to tease it out a bit to see if people would be excited about TMSM coming back, and to my delight, they were. We told people that on December 1, 2012, we were coming back. And we did. Bigger, better, stronger. The Main Street Mouse was back again, and I was humbled and grateful at the welcome response we received. From that point on, things became a blur. All of a sudden, businesses were approaching me about advertising and sponsorship, and I had no idea what to do about that. Would having advertisers change how we did things? Do sponsors get a say so in what I put in my blog posts? I didn't want that. I was still finding my own footing on how to proceed and I needed to do it on my own terms.

About a month went by and we had our first advertiser, a travel agency. Another agency messaged me and said they'd double what that company was paying to advertise with us, but I declined. It wasn't about the money, it was about being true to my word and keeping my integrity intact. Within a few months, things got bigger and bigger, more businesses started to approach us, and I wasn't prepared for it.

With success comes negativity, too. In the Disney community, you ask? Oh, yes. One would think I lived in a hole somewhere, because I had no idea how tough and competitive the website business could be, but I was about to learn. People came out of the woodwork, wanting to "help." Some, long-time Main Streeters, yes, they truly did want to help. Others, meaning others in the business, well, not so much. Our Facebook page likes were growing by the thousands each week, and the talk started. People thought we had to be cheating our way to the top somehow, but that wasn't the case; it was all organic, all good content which caused positive word of mouth. I couldn't understand how anyone could think spreading magic and having a good sense of community was a bad thing. Well, when they view you as competition, that's where things change. I didn't know anyone, didn't follow other sites, and I still don't. My parents always taught me to keep my eyes on my own paper, and focus on what I'm doing, not what everyone else is doing. It's proven to be solid advice that I still follow to this day.

In life, when you have people coming at you in a negative way, you have two options. You can cave in and give up. Or you can take that negativity and bullying and use it as fuel. There's an old philosophy that you must be doing something right if you're getting people talking or having folks trying to bring you down. I chose the second option, but it wasn't easy. It was downright hard. Very hard. I quickly found out that I didn't have thick skin when it came to these things, and there were many times I'd sit at my computer and cry. How sad is that? Even sadder, there were also times that my stomach would churn before even logging into my computer because I never knew what kind of mess was waiting for me. There was a period where every morning when I'd wake up, I'd have to go clean up spam and vulgar images on our business Facebook page that our "competitors" left overnight. In the Disney community? Can't be? Yes, and it's shocking and something many don't speak about. It's not all pixie dust and Dole Whips, trust me. So, what's a girl to do? Quit? Heck no! Do better, that's what you do. Press on. It's the better road.

One thing that set us apart was the personal blogs. When I write, I write from the heart. I want our readers to feel like we're just sitting at a table having coffee together, just friends having a chat. It is what it is, and keeping things on a personal level is so important, and people seem to appreciate that. Humor is also something that we did in the beginning. Posting funny pics on our Facebook page also helped it grow. When you're building a following, you also have to keep things fresh and change things up. Try new things. We did member-of-the-month giveaways, a Halloween costume contest, and one of our biggest ideas, TMSM Idol, where we had members send in videos of them singing "Let It Go" for a chance to win a Disney gift card. The singing contest was fun. It was important to us to not only give people the opportunity to interact and have a positive outlet, but also for us to give back to them as a thank you for following along with us.

We had our ups and downs, but all in all, things were going well. Our "hobby" was growing into something much bigger than I ever could have imagined. At that point, I was just happy that our readers were happy. In the fall of 2013, one of my articles got picked up by a radio station in another state, then shared again at another news outlet. TMSM picked up speed yet again, and for the first time, I thought, 'Maybe we really have something here?'

CHAPTER FOUR

I've Got a Dream

In the midst of our website growing by leaps and bounds, we ran into a new hardship. My husband, who also worked in Detroit, was let go from his job due to downsizing. In southeast Michigan, this was becoming an epidemic for so many families. Businesses were either being bought out, closing, or they were making cutbacks. There were a lot of people in the same boat as us, but we did have TMSM picking up steam. It was decision time. We were lucky enough to get a severance from Scott's job, so during that time, he looked for work and we really gave TMSM a push. We figured, if this was going to turn into an actual business, now would be the time to put our all into it and see what could happen.

Times were hard for a while. That Christmas we had little under the tree, just what we could do for the boys, and it wasn't much. I was so sad, but determined to make some changes. Something had to give. We did the TMSM Idol contest in early 2014, and at that point, we were in discussions on what we should do. The contest was the extra push that we needed, being that it did so well, and our reader numbers were fast on the rise. Now what? I knew that running a Disney site from Michigan wasn't easy, but it wasn't my "job" when I started it, so I managed. TMSM went from hobby to work, and I knew if I wanted it to do even better, we needed to make some changes. We had talked many times about moving to Florida. Sure, it would be nice to live among the palm trees and sunshine, and be close to Disney, but would we ever actually make the move? I was scared, and to me, it was just dreaming.

One snowy day, while we were sitting home doing site work, my dad stopped by. My parents came over to our house often to visit; they only lived ten minutes away, so it wasn't a surprise. The surprise was what he wanted to talk to me about. Let me preface this by saying that I'm very close to my family. Very. We always have lived near each other, done family dinners, barbecues in the summertime, everything that you'd hope to do with a close-knit family unit. That was us. Not just my parents, but extended family, too. Grandparents, aunts, uncles, cousins ... you get the idea. That was a huge reason why we never moved south, because I couldn't imagine living away from the people I loved most.

My parents are retired and run a soup kitchen for the local Salvation Army twice a week, so I assumed he was bringing us lunch, but he wasn't. My dad sat down and said that he needed to talk to me. He could see how TMSM was blossoming and was so proud of me. As hard as it was for him to say, my father told me I had his blessing to follow my Disney dreams and get the heck out of Michigan. There was nothing to keep me there, other than family. The economy was bad, my health wasn't the greatest, the cold weather was rough on my younger son Aidan's asthma ... he told me to go. My first thought was, why would he say that? Wouldn't he miss us? My dad said he and my mom talked about it, and it would be foolish of me to stay in Michigan and not pursue my dreams. They didn't want to see us leave, but they also could see the potential there and told me I had to at least give it a shot. After a lot of tears, I knew deep down that my parents were right, as hard as that was. If they, being as close to us as they are, could see the potential benefit of us moving to Florida, I needed to look at it seriously too. I thanked him, and said we'd give it some thought.

Truthfully, we had already been thinking about it, but I'm not sure how serious we were. It's easy to want to move out of state when there's snow on the ground and the windchill temperature is 20 below zero. It's easy to talk to your friends in Florida and hear what's going on in Disney and wish you could be there. But that's a dream only, right? Or is it? I'm one of those indecisive people that can't choose what I want for dinner, let alone make a life-altering decision. Being assertive and "brave" was not my thing. Sure, I had been through hell and back in years prior, between health issues, personal issues, and money issues, but I pulled through. I never thought I was brave or strong, I just knew that you have to do what you have to do when there is no other choice.

But now, I had a choice. What in the world was I going to do? I hate change, I'm co-dependent on my family, I don't think I can do something crazy like this and pick up and move across the country. I had a lot of thinking to do.

During my thinking period, as I call it, I was desperate for signs. Again, I'm the girl who didn't know what movie to see or what kind of ice cream to order, so I needed an extra push. Yes, I had my parents backing me, which was a blessing, but I wasn't scared and didn't want to commit to doing something like this. Not yet.

My birthday is in February, and as usual, we went to my parents house for a party with all our family and friends. The usual pizza, cake, and ice cream were on hand ... and wine, another staple for our family get-togethers. I remember sitting in my parent's basement looking around at everyone there, and my heart physically hurt. None of them knew what I was pondering, but inside, I couldn't stop thinking about it. Could I actually leave them? I know moving to Florida isn't like moving to Europe, but it's far enough. Too far from the people in that room. It wasn't just birthdays, it was pool parties in the summer, it was family dinners, holidays, just dropping by to say hello for no special reason. Could I give that up? I felt guilty for even thinking about moving away. I'm not sure anyone thought that I'd go. I didn't think that I'd go. It was torture. I remember that birthday in particular because I started to look at everyone differently. I realized just how much I love my family and how blessed I was to have them..

Besides my extended family and my close friends, I needed to consider others when it came to moving to Florida. The biggest factor: my boys, Andrew and Aidan. Some parents do what they're going to do, and assume that kids are resilient and will adjust to whatever decision is made. I couldn't do that. The happiness of my boys far outweighed my own wants. No parent is perfect, but one thing I always tried to be was a good mother. My boys are my heart and soul, and if they're not happy, I'm not happy. I had made mistakes in my life, we all have, but where the kids are concerned, I was determined to do right by them. We can't change the past, all we can do is do better in the future.

I sat them down, and told them I was considering moving us to Florida, just to test the waters. If they got upset or cried, then there was no way we'd go. What I got was the exact opposite. The boys got excited, and said they wanted to move. I was surprised by that. So, of course, I had to play devil's advocate, to make sure they realize what moving south will entail. I brought up the harsh facts, like moving away from family, switching schools, finding a new place to live, not being able to see our loved ones as much as we wanted to. All of it. Even taking all that into consideration, they boys wanted to go. They were excited. That was one sign I was looking for, and I got it.

Still, I kept looking for signs. I'd get mail from Disney, and would think, 'Oh, maybe that's a sign?' Or see a Disney commercial ... same thing, that's a sign. I think I asked the kids every single day, "Are you SURE you want to move to Florida?" They answered the same every single time: yes.

One day I was talking to Andrew in his room about moving, and he said "Mom, I think you're the one who doesn't want to leave, because we keep saying yes, but you keep asking." Pretty darn smart for a kid. He was spot on, it was me. I was the one who was scared and filled with doubt. That was a pivotal moment. Enough waiting for signs or asking everyone I know what we should do. After a lot of tears and prayers, I finally agreed; we were moving to Florida. We have to try now, or we never will.

CHAPTER FIVE

Moving Forward

So, we're moving to Florida! Hooray! Now what?

There is so much to do and so much to consider when you make the huge decision to move your family roughly 1200 miles away from home. I wasn't sure where to begin. It was late winter, still cold outside, I thought I had plenty of time to make a plan. I really didn't. The goal was to be out of our house and on the road to Florida once the boys got out of school in June. I seriously don't know what I was thinking. Do I just work better under pressure? Was I somehow in a subconscious way trying to sabotage my plan? Maybe. It's all a blur. We started getting rid of extra things, donating clothes and other items to Goodwill, just to see if we could make any headway purging the house for the big move. Also, in the meantime, I was online looking into rental houses not far from Walt Disney World. Again, in the back of my head, I thought if we couldn't find a house, then it wasn't meant to be, and that would be my sign to stay put in Michigan. I was looking for signs on all sides, good or bad.

Thanks to the power of social media and the internet, I found out that a rental house about 10 minutes from Disney was going to be available in June. June! Perfect! I didn't want to get too excited until Scott was able to talk to the landlord to see if it's something we could do, or if he'd even want us as tenants. They spoke on the phone for about 45 minutes, and I was pacing around the house. There I was making deals in my head again, waiting for that sign. Scott got off the phone and I could barely breathe waiting for him to tell me how it went. He just smiled and said, "He's putting the rental agreement in the mail, we got the house." We were thrilled! Things were falling into place, fast. Everything we were waiting on, every sign I was holding out for, was happening. Was God telling me to stop being a chicken and just go for it? I was starting to think so ... and it was terrifying. We weren't even sure where this house was; we had only seen pictures. Were we crazy to pack up and move to a house that we haven't even walked through? Possibly. Something inside me was telling me to just go and it would all be okay, and I had to rely on those feelings. The rent was double what we paid in Michigan, I wasn't sure how we were going to get things done by June, but we signed the paperwork and put our moving plan into place. Yes, this was happening. We were moving to Main Street, U.S.A. Disney World, here we come!

But first, a few things needed to be done. Well, a lot of things.

Up until this point, I hadn't really told too many people of our plans. I didn't want to, because if I did, that made it too real. After making an agreement with the landlord, my first thought after the excitement wore off was, 'Shoot, things just got real,' and I knew that it was time to push forward, get our packing done, make arrangements, and put it all out there. I was terrified. People tell me I'm brave, but honestly, the whole time I was packing, putting down deposits, making arrangements for this and that ... in my head I was still thinking, 'I can't believe I'm doing this.' and would tell myself that if things fell through, it would be okay and I'd know that it wasn't meant to be. I was fine with that. Scared, but going through the motions regardless.

There was so much that I had to do, as well as there being a lot to learn. I had only moved once, not including moving out of my parents' house when I got married in my twenties. Even then, I had bought my grandparents' house which was only ten minutes from my mom and dad, and it was a house that was a second home for me, so the move wasn't a huge adjustment. A few years back we moved out of that house and were living someplace new, still only ten minutes away, and in the same city. We had moved into a house that was a bit more updated, needed less work, and we really fixed it up cute. And now we're leaving that cute house. We had put a lot of work into it: paint, fixtures, landscaping. It looked awesome! And we're moving? I must have been losing my mind. See what self doubt can do?

I liked my house, but we had only been there two years so it wasn't "home." I didn't think I'd have as hard of a time leaving it as I did the other house we had, the one that my grandparents raised my mother in, the one that I brought my own babies home to. Now that one was a heartbreaker. If I could get through that move, I could certainly let go of this house easier. At least that was my hope.

And so it began ... time to purge our house of things we didn't need, and start deciding what we were keeping and taking with us on our big move. Easier said than done. Also, it was time to let the world know we were moving. I couldn't easily back out once I told our readers that we were moving, so it was a huge step. So much to do in a short time, and we had to get moving. Literally.

I made the announcement to our following roughly a month before it was time to move, and the response was exciting. What I didn't expect was the interest people would have in the moving process and how they wanted to come along with us on this journey, so to speak. I've always done different themes on our site on certain days, so I decided to do a "Moving to Main Street" blog each Wednesday night, to update everyone on the process. This was also a way for me to journal our experience while keeping people in the loop.

So, it was May, we were moving by mid June, and I wasn't ready. Now what? Well, we had just moved two years prior, and I "thought" I had already gotten rid of a lot of thing I no longer used. I thought wrong. Once I started going through closets and things, I felt so overwhelmed. Not only did I have a ton of stuff still, it was stuff that I didn't want to part with. I'm one of those people who puts value on just about everything. For instance, when I was little, I didn't want my mom to put the Christmas tree on the curb after the holidays, because I felt sorry for it. I'm not even kidding. I did get better about things, and fully realize that inanimate objects don't have feelings, but it was me. I had the feelings, and everything meant something. Did I mention I hate change? So much so that it's paralyzing some-times. I started with the front coat closet; I mean, there can't be *that* much in a coat closet that I need to keep, right? Wrong. Living in Michigan your entire life means that you have more than one winter coat or pair of boots. Actually, I had about seven coats and more winter boots and shoes than I could count. Some I never wore, but that's beside the point. I didn't want to part with *any* of it. Was it denial? Maybe. Okay, probably. It's hard to explain how much I had to push myself into making changes and adjusting to things that I'm not totally comfortable with, like getting rid of things. As I sat on the floor, surrounded by coats and adorable boots that I still had plans to wear, I had to level with myself. In Florida, am I going to need a handful of wool coats? Sure, it gets cold, but not snowy or below zero, so the answer was no. I made a deal with myself to keep two of them (maybe three), and the rest were going to Goodwill. Now about those boots ... sigh. If I'm being honest, I didn't part with many shoes; instead, I got extra packing boxes. Most of those cold weather shoes are still in boxes in my garage. In Florida, folks mostly wear sandals or flip flops, not snow boots, but I did the best I could at the time.

One of the hardest parts with moving and purging things we didn't need was going through the boys' rooms. Talk about sentimental. When it comes to my boys, I hang on to everything. From baby clothes, to pictures they made me in preschool; I'm so bad with that. I started making a pile of extra clothes and toys that I could give to charity, but some things I just couldn't get rid of. After many instances of seeing me sitting on the floor crying, my husband finally said we'd get extra boxes. He wasn't going to make me give up things that I wasn't ready to give up. This comes back to bite me later.

Part of the issue with going through things in our home is dealing with the memories attached. They aren't just "things," they are part of us. In my heart I knew I couldn't keep it all, but as I tell people, I'm a work in progress, and sometimes baby steps are necessary. Once the ball got rolling, it was easier to purge.

It was now three weeks before we headed south, and we were nowhere near ready. If you looked around our house, you'd never know we were moving. Decorations were still on the wall, dishes were still in cupboards, nothing looked out of place. Part of me wondered if I was dragging my feet out of fear. Yes, fear. For some, moving closer to Disney is a dream come true and is fun and exciting. But it's also scary. I've never lived anywhere else, and change is rough. I still couldn't believe I was doing this. I've always dreamed of moving to Florida, but I feared the unknown. I love Florida, I was always sad to leave once our vacations were over, I felt like I left part of my heart in Florida every time. But, the other half of my heart was in Michigan, with family and friends. Where is the balance? Could I *find* said balance once I moved, and if so, how?

I had to stop procrastinating and keep pushing forward. Time was running out. I had boxes of crafting supplies that I hadn't touched in months, but I kept saying, maybe one day I'll need it. Same with decorations. Since I didn't know what our new house really looked like, I didn't want to get rid of pictures and other decorations, because ... what if I need them? Well, people don't decorate the same in the south, and I could have gotten rid of more than I did.

In the midst of packing, we had a week where both boys had their birthdays, plus my parents had their yearly Memorial Day BBQ. We always got together with family for holidays and birthdays. Always. Summertime at my parents' house is always a lot of fun. They have a beautiful pool in their yard, and it seems that all of my family gathers there when the weather is good, to relax and socialize.

That year on Memorial Day, I sat with my feet in my parents' pool, looking around their beautiful yard and watching everyone having fun, and I could feel the tears welling up under my sunglasses. It would have been easier to get ready to leave Michigan in the winter time, when the weather is bad and makes me miserable. Summer time in Michigan was family time, and I felt like I was going to miss out. That just about killed me. My main solace was that I knew I could come back for Christmas and other events, and if my parents really missed us or wanted to get away, they were welcome to come to Florida to visit. I had to come to terms with that and rationalize in my mind that this would work, or I knew I'd back out. Moving to pursue your Disney dreams sounds crazy to some, but it's also exciting, and frightening. Just a mixed bag of emotions ... and I had to deal with those emotions because time was running out.

We needed extra money for moving, so I decided to have a yard sale. Great idea, right? In theory it was, but the driveway looked like a thrift store made a drop at my house. The first two days went well. The third day, a Sunday, traffic was slow, and I still had a ton of things that I didn't truly need. I was actually giving away things to people who came to the yard sale. One woman told me her mom was in the late stages of lung cancer, and her daughters needed dresses for the services and such. I went through my clothes and gave her dresses, shoes, jewelry, anything I could find. Another person was looking for items for her daycare, so I gave her boxes of my crafting and art supplies. Giving things away does the heart good, and I can't even begin to explain how great of a feeling that was. Later in the afternoon, we decided to put some of what was left on the curb with a sign for people to just take what they wanted. A lady drove by and said she needed items for a local shelter, and I loaded up her van for free. Another person was looking for items they could use at the animal shelter, and again, I told them to take as much as they needed. In addition to that, we donated about 20 boxes of household items and clothes to the local Salvation Army for donation. Not only was it satisfying to give things away to those who were in need, it helped me out, too—less things to fit in the truck. Our theory was that we could always replace things later once we moved, and to take only what we absolutely needed. Even doing that, we had a huge amount to pack. Moving across the country is so stressful, but we were doing what we needed to do. I think part of me was in denial, because doing this was not like me. I never venture out of my comfort zone, but now I was. It was almost time.

That final week before the move I was numb, just going through the motions to get things done and not thinking about it too much. In hindsight, I believe it was a coping mechanism. If I just did what I needed to do, then I might not be such a mess. That last weekend, though, I was a mess. We got rid of as much as I could part with, and I thought we did good ... until we picked up the moving truck. Even with all the stuff I donated, I still had too much. How could that be? We made 10 car trips to Goodwill, had a garage sale, threw out a lot of junk, and I still didn't make the cut for space. We started packing the truck, and it began to look like pieces of a puzzle. We were fitting items in every little space, to the point that there was absolutely *no* room left. My parents hired a neighbor kid and a friend to help load the truck, but we were maxed out. My mom and dad stood with me in the garage, and I started to cry. I had purged about all I could, and I finally hit my breaking point. So, instead of making me get rid of more of my belongings, they told me to leave what's left in the garage. Thank God. You see, my house in Michigan wasn't being sold, they were going to rent it for us for a year, in case we didn't like Florida and changed our minds. That was my safety net, so some of my things could be left behind.

Knowing my house was still there made it so much easier to cope with the move. It's funny the things we tell ourselves when we have to find ways to be brave and do things we normally wouldn't do. So that was it, that's what I told myself. Florida was like a year-long vacation, and I could always come back home.

It worked for me and I was sticking to that.

CHAPTER SIX

See Ya Real Soon

Once the truck was packed to the max, we had two days left. We were heading to Florida on Monday morning, so on Sunday my family had one last pool party for us to say goodbye. Well, not goodbye, just see ya real soon, that's the Disney way. That afternoon, my entire family was there, as well as a few of my best friends. We had a good time, but it was bittersweet. As the afternoon went on, I had a feeling of dread, because I knew that they would start leaving and we'd have to bid our farewells. I was going to be coming back home for Christmas, but that was six months away, and in my lifetime, I've never been away from these people for that long. To some, that may sound strange, but to us, that was our lives. We were close with everyone, and we liked it that way. One by one, they went home at the end of the evening, and each person got a longer hug than usual, along with some tears. Six months, I could do six months, right? It won't be so bad. But it felt *bad*. You just never know what can happen, and I value my family so much, I didn't want to miss time with them. I'm lucky enough to have one grandparent left, and each time I see her I cherish it. Saying goodbye to her about broke me. My parents were driving down with us to Florida, so I didn't have to worry about that part yet. Once everyone was gone, Scott and I went home, to spend our last night at our house. The boys stayed with my mom and dad because their rooms were empty. We had to sleep on the floor, with only a few things left in the house. We didn't sleep much, at least I didn't. Not only was I uncomfortable on the floor, I was scared.

About 5:00 in the morning, we closed the doors to the house for the last time and got in the truck to head to my parents' house. I looked back at our porch, and tried to burn that moment in my mind. I needed to remember, I needed to have things to help me cope. As we drove, I looked at everything a little longer on that ten-minute drive. Heck, even the McDonald's we went to every Sunday, I was taking it all in. When we got to my parents' house, they were in the doorway, waiting. The boys had been up for a while; they were too excited to sleep, just as if we were going on a Disney vacation. Same concept, but we weren't coming back, not for a while anyhow. My dad was going to drive with Scott in the moving truck, and my mom, the boys, the dog and the cats were driving in our truck with me. Before leaving, we all held hands and said a prayer for a safe trip, gave everyone a hug, then said let's do this. There we were, taking the biggest leap of faith that we've ever taken. All those months of worrying, preparing, praying, second guessing ... it was all over with, and we were on our way.

Usually, the trip to Disney takes seventeen to eighteen hours. This time, though, we had the moving truck to contend with, so we weren't driving as fast. Between the truck, the kids needing to stop for bathroom breaks, my dad wanting to stop at Waffle House, and getting gas in both vehicles, it was to going be a longer trip this time.

We planned to stop for the night in Georgia, as there was no way were going to make it driving straight through to Florida. We were tired, and although my husband and father had a nice quiet ride, my mom and I were ready to stop for the night since we had kids and animals with us. Speaking of animals, one of our pets, Punkin, wasn't in the greatest shape. She was older, but she was my eldest son Andrew's cat, and I didn't want him to have to leave her behind. I knew her health was failing, but she seemed well enough to travel. When we stopped for the night, our younger cat was fine, but the older one was looking very weak and sick. We needed to get her some water and food and let her rest, so I was so glad we stopped. My parents went out to dinner, but the rest of stayed at the hotel and got fast food. The next morning we hit the road early, because we had a goal in mind of getting to the house by mid afternoon. I was sick of driving. We all felt that way; we were ready to begin the next chapter. Once we crossed the Florida state line, everyone started to get excited. Our journey was almost over. The excitement got even greater when we started to see billboards for Walt Disney World. This was actually happening.

CHAPTER SEVEN

A Whole New World

As we got closer to our new home, I was full of different emotions. I was tired, grouchy, and sore from the drive; I didn't even know where we were going. Scott had put the address into the GPS on his phone, so I was following him. I knew my way around Orlando, for the most part. I knew the highway, I knew Disney property, I even knew how to get to Universal Studios. But I didn't know where we were going to be living.

When the truck made the turn into the subdivision, my heart started pounding. My mom even said, "I hope this place isn't a dump!" We laughed, but I was hoping it wasn't, too. The landlord had sent pictures, but there weren't many of them, so I was going into this blindly. He told us he painted the walls and put in wood flooring, but that's all I knew.

Conveniently, our landlord was pulling up at the same time we were. He worked for Disney and just left his job to come bring us the keys and show us around. The outside of the house looked the same as it did in the photos. One concern down, the rest to go. As we walked up to the front door, I said a prayer: "Please God, let this be a place we can call home." This was it. Even if it wasn't great, I knew we had to make things work. My parents felt the same. They knew they would have a harder time leaving us in Florida if the house we had wasn't a good place to be.

We walked inside, and all my worries faded away. In Michigan, the houses tend to be boxy, with smaller rooms, shorter ceilings, etc. This house in Florida was an open concept, quite spacious, and very nice. The feeling of relief was overwhelming. We walked through the house, taking it all in. My dad followed me into the back room and he hugged me and cried, saying this place was so much better for us than what we had. This could be a home for us, and he was thankful. The boys were quickly negotiating who got which room. My little guy, Aidan, wanted to know where the basement was. Well, kiddo, in Florida, we have no basement. Actually, the no-basement change was a good one, because in Michigan, our basement leaked. That won't be an issue here. The kids had their own bathroom, we had a bigger kitchen, and a big selling feature for the kids: a pool. I used to buy kiddie pools for them every year, as part of their birthday presents. Now we had one that I don't have to throw out each season. All in all, we were happy. The blind leap of faith was good so far, and I was thankful. Now the fun part ... unloading the truck.

If you're thinking of making the move from the north to sunny Florida, there are so many things you'll want to know that you may not have considered. I'll cover all of that. First things first, let's go back to that lack of basement. Up north, where do people store extra items? The basement, of course! Basements are for storage, play rooms, pool tables, social gatherings, Christmas decorations ... you get the idea. As we were unloading the truck, I was quickly seeing where a basement could have come in handy. The square footage in the new house is all on one floor. The closets are bigger, but as far as storage goes, there just isn't any. Extra boxes had to go in the garage. But what about the bugs? Don't you know Florida is known for huge bugs? At that point, we had no choice, and I knew we'd be buying bug spray in the near future. And what about all those decorations I saved? Well, open concept means less walls, so a lot of those items stayed in boxes, too. Being that I've never lived in Florida or known someone in the family who has, we were learning as we went.

Now, back to boxy rooms. Our Michigan furniture fit perfectly in our living room. The living room in the new house was much more open, so the couch felt like it was set up a football field's length away from the television. I'm exaggerating, but you get the idea. Decorating really *is* different down here. Everything is set up in quite an opposite way from what we're used to. My parents weren't heading back to Michigan for three days, so I had to use my time, especially with my mom, to put things in order. We had the same furniture and decor, but it looked so different here. The boys' rooms were easy; their beds and other furniture fit just fine. They were excited to set up their rooms, so we worked on that first. We made much more progress that first night than I anticipated. We got boxes unpacked, kitchen items put away, beds set up ... all was going pretty well, minus the pool. But my dad wasn't happy....

Let me give you a little back story. Ever since I was a little girl, my parents always had a pool in their yard. My dad took pride in keeping the pool a nice sparkling blue by checking the chemicals, ph levels, all the fun stuff that I don't understand. He's always been a pro when it comes to swimming pools. When my dad went to check out the pool at the new house, he gasped. He might have even grabbed his chest. The landlord said they hadn't had time to get the pool ready for us, but we didn't realize what that meant until we got a better look. The pool water was a lovely shade of green, had chips in the bottom along with dirt, and a dead frog and huge bug were floating in it. Needless to say, my dad wasn't having any part of that, and was going to make it his mission to fix that mess before he went home. So my mom was helping on the inside of the house, and my dad was playing pool man. All was going fine thus far, but I knew my time with them was limited and there was so much to do.

Another aspect of moving across the country and starting to unpack what's left from your previous life is realizing how much you don't have, things that you usually take for granted. Like food. Or toilet paper. Or dish soap. I got rid of a lot of things from the old house, things that I knew could be replaced, because as I said our moving truck was full. After we spent some time unpacking, we thought it might be a good idea to send someone to the store to get some basics for the house. It's all such a blur. That first day, I was tired, emotional, excited, scared ... all balled up into one. I still couldn't believe I had made this move. Somehow, I needed to figure out how to make this place our new normal, even if it meant just getting some pop (yes, in Michigan we say "pop" instead of "soda"), chips, breakfast foods, and other essentials in the house.

Because of how many times I had been to the Orlando area, I knew where the major attractions were located, but I didn't know my new neighborhood or its surroundings at all. Where was a Target? Walmart? What is this Publix place I see everywhere? And what the heck is a WaWa, and why is it so busy all the time? Talk about being out of my element. Thank God for Google! We got the truck unpacked pretty fast, got some groceries and supplies, and made good progress turning the new place into a home. I honestly don't remember going to bed that first night.

The next day, we got more items unpacked, and put boxes in the garage. Again, no basement, no storage. Amid all the unpacking, we realized that Andrew's cat really was on the decline, and we had a horrible decision to make. You know that decision; most of us have had to face it at one point or another. Change is hard, and I didn't want it to be hard for the boys. I knew the cat wasn't in the best shape, but we had to try. My dad called around to get her in to see a veterinarian, and we spoke to Andrew about the possibility that Punkin was just too sick to get better at this point. He knew, and he wanted to go with my dad to the vet. As they were getting ready to go, we wrapped Punkin up in a towel, she was so weak, and we gave her lots of love. My dad told me to stay home with my mom and keep working, that he would be fine with Andrew. They were gone about an hour, and when they came back, all they had was the towel and Punkin's collar. My heart broke. It was just too much, all of it. Moving, dealing with unpacking, new people stopping by, the cat getting sick, and knowing that in two days my parents were leaving. So yes, I sat on my couch, the one that's a football field's length away from the TV, and I just cried. And cried, and cried. It was needed. Just like that, the self doubt came creeping back in. Oh, and guilt, let's not forget guilt. I uprooted my family, pushed for this new adventure, and now I killed the cat. I didn't, really, she was very old and sick, but in my head, that was my fault, too. Sometimes we want so badly to make things perfect for those we love, that when those efforts fall short, we take it hard. Really hard. Is it irrational? Maybe. But raw emotions are what they are, and I'm thankful my mother was still there to help. What was I going to do without her? Or my dad? I seriously didn't know, but I couldn't focus on that or I'd ruin the time we had left before they went back to Michigan.

After a few days of hard work, tears, and emotional exhaustion, we decided to go out the night before my parents left. We didn't have Disney passes yet. We didn't have *anything* yet. Mom and Dad love Jimmy Buffett, so the only logical solution was to go to Universal's City Walk and have dinner at Margaritaville. We *all* deserved a margarita after the week we had! I hadn't been to City Walk in years, and I missed it. My dad said that he could tell I was "in my element" there. Theme parks, attractions, those were were my things. They always have been. It was exciting. We walked up to Margaritaville to put our names on the list for dinner, and lo and behold, the inside of the dining area was closed for a private event. Not kidding. The outside was open, so we made the best of things and got our cheeseburgers in paradise and frozen concoctions out on the patio. Come to find out, Jimmy Buffett was having an event in there, but we didn't see him. After dinner, we went into the gift shop. My parents were going to a Buffett concert in Detroit later that summer and wanted to buy some new shirts. As my dad was at the register, he was chatting it up with the cashier. She asked if they were on vacation, he said no, that his daughter just moved down here for work. Then she asks my dad, "Is your daughter Michele from The Main Street Mouse?" He lit up like a Christmas tree and called me over there. Little did we know, this nice lady followed our site, and it was very humbling to talk to her. That's the first person I met down here who follows what we do, and it wasn't even *at* Disney. Go figure. For my dad, I think it gave him a little consolation to realize that what we did really was a great thing, and we were going to be alright. At least we hoped so.

Then, before we knew it, my parents were leaving for the airport. We had been on quite an adventure together in the past week. Between our going-away party, traveling two days, unpacking and setting up shop, and squeezing a little fun time in ... it was time to say goodbye. Maybe not goodbye, but another "see ya real soon." In my entire life, I have never gone very long without seeing family. I think the longest was maybe a week. Maybe. It was June, and they weren't coming back to visit until mid September. That's too long. How was I going to handle that? I couldn't think that far in advance, and just had to deal with what was in front of me, which was the people who brought me into this world and made me the person that I am today. The people who have supported me no matter what, through good times and bad. It's always been unconditional with my parents; they always have my back, and now they were leaving.

Before heading out, there were a lot of hugs and a lot of tears. It was so hard. One thing they left me with, that made a difference, was telling me how proud they were of us taking such a huge leap. No matter how old you get, hearing your parents tell you they're proud of you is always so good to hear. Sometimes it's really needed, too; that day it sure was. We gave our last hugs and "I love you's" and they were gone.

I continued to cry for a bit after they left. Could I do this without family here? Was I going to have a meltdown eventually, not knowing anyone? Once again, I had to shove those negative thoughts out of my head, because reality was setting in, and there was so much still to do.

CHAPTER EIGHT

Now What?

So, we're almost fully unpacked, my family is on their way home, and it's just the hubby and kids and I. Alone. Now what? Well, we had TMSM work to attend to, and I quickly found out that the new house was basically a dead zone for cell phone and Wifi reception. That was *not* going to work. To get online, reliably, I had to drive the car up to the main road. To say I was stressed is an understatement. When your job is virtual, you can't go without technology for long. Was I going to have to run TMSM from Starbucks? This wasn't good. Eventually the cable company came out and hooked us up, but it wasn't right away.

Another not-so-fun aspect of moving far from home, besides learning the area, not having family, not having internet, and so on, is getting the house set up, bill wise. We had a nest egg of money when we moved. We thought it would last us a bit, but we were basing that on Michigan costs, not Florida costs. I learned the hard way that the cost of living was much higher here in Florida. I called to have the electric company change the service over to my name, and they told me there was a $500 deposit. That felt like a punch in the gut. We didn't have that kind of money. After paying for the truck, gas, hotel, food, household items, and cable, among other things, now we were having to put out another huge chunk of money. Self-doubt returned. Moving is expensive, yes, but moving across the country is even worse. If you are considering making a big move like this, check out the cost for utilities and other essentials ahead of time; it may save you some heartache. Everything has activation fees here, and they're not small fees. We had a certain amount of money set aside for different things, and it was quickly going.

One thing that we purposely saved up for was our Walt Disney World annual passes. Since we moved here to expand our Disney business, the passes were an expense that we needed to make. It's for work. Fun work, but work nonetheless. At that point, reality really hadn't set in; it felt like we were on vacation. We had only been there less than a week, and we went to Downtown Disney to get our passes, so it really *was* the same feeling you get when you're just vacationing. It was hard to believe we weren't on vacation, that this was real life. In my head, it seemed like within a week or so, we'd be leaving the land of Mickey Mouse and palm trees, and heading back to Michigan. Not the case. Having the Disney theme parks so close was a good thing; they were a great distraction from the scary parts of what we'd just done. How was I going to feel in a few weeks, though? Would I finally get it in my head that this wasn't vacation, it's reality, and I'm not going back to Michigan anytime soon?

The goal was to accept things for what they are and adjust. My focus was to make sure the boys were happy and adjusted, too. It's a big deal, and when you're like me and aren't used to taking big steps, it's quite intimidating. Vacation mode was okay for now, with work in between. However we needed to adjust, it was fine. As long as the kids were happy, I was happy.

CHAPTER NINE

Disney from a Different Perspective

After getting settled, it was time to relax. We were here for over a week before we really ventured out, and since we just got those Disney annual passes, I wanted to put them to good use. Around 7:00 one evening, after a day of working, we finally went to my favorite Disney park, Magic Kingdom. It had been almost three years since we'd been there, and we were excited to go. There were so many times that I only wished we could go to Disney, but life got in the way and plans had to change. Now, we lived so close to my happy place, it was still surreal to think that this wasn't vacation, but that first time it sure felt that way. We got inside the park and my heart was full. Seeing the sights that I longed to see, smelling the scents of Main Street, U.S.A., watching people taking photos in front of Cinderella Castle … I just had to take it all in. We took a few pictures, went over to Tomorrowland to see one of my cast member friends, then had to hurry to get to our first FastPass. The MagicBand technology was new, so it was our first time using the bands rather than a paper FastPass. Our first ride on our new adventure was Big Thunder Mountain Railroad. The kids love that coaster; so do I. Since we got to the park later in the day, we had to move things along to make the most of our time.

After Big Thunder Mountain, we took a walk over to the new Fantasyland. The expansion was just finished a few months prior, so the whole area was new to us. Sure, we covered the details of the expansion for the site, from Michigan, but now I got to experience it. We were all impressed with the new area. From the Seven Dwarfs

Mine Train, to the Tangled restrooms, it was all beautiful. I have a true affection for Tangled, so I spent more time than usual taking pictures of the lanterns and getting photos of the purple swirls and suns painted on the wall. We rode Mine Train for the first time that evening, too, and it was also a hit. After that, we headed to our usual dining place when we vacationed, Cosmic Ray's, to grab a bite to eat, then over to Space Mountain. We were cramming a whole lot into one evening, but it was great.

What I looked forward to the most this "first" night was seeing Wishes, the Magic Kingdom's classic fireworks show. Everyone loves Wishes. We high tailed it to find a place near the front of the castle, and got there just in time to watch the show. As the festivities went on, probably within the first 30 seconds, tears began to run down my face. Yes, I usually do cry when I see Wishes, but this time it felt different. I always wished that I could live close to Disney World, and that wish had finally come true. There was just a whole new meaning for the experience now. Behind me were my sons, and seeing the look of wonder and happiness on their faces was the best thing. Often times in life we take moments for granted and we tend not to savor them. That's not me. When the situation involves Disney in combination with my kids, I'm like a sponge. I try to soak it all in, take mental pictures of what's going on at that time, because I never want to forget. Kids grow so fast, and special moments turn into memories, so taking time to reflect, even if it's on the spot, is a good idea.

So there we were, in front of my favorite castle, at my favorite place, with my favorite people. It doesn't get much better than that. We had talked about the "what if's" of moving to Florida so many times, and how great it would be, and we were there. Yes, there were tears, but happy tears. I'll never forget that.

Once Wishes was done, we kept pushing on to cram more activities into our fun-filled evening. Even though it was late and the sun had set, it was still really hot outside, so we went on Splash Mountain. I had forgotten how hot Florida can be in the summertime, even at night. That took some getting used to. After Splash Mountain, we went on my personal favorite attraction, the Haunted Mansion, then my husband's favorite, Pirates of the Caribbean. We did a lot. Not bad for a first visit to Disney as Florida residents!

One of the high points of the evening came as we were leaving. I didn't need to feel sad, as I usually did. In the past, leaving the Magic

Kingdom at night was always rough because I didn't know when I'd be able to come back. Now I knew that I could come back and visit more often, no need to feel bad anymore.

In the next week or so, we continued to adjust to our new home. We did get in some Disney time, too, of course. One afternoon, we went back to the Magic Kingdom to see the Festival of Fantasy Parade. At that point, being that it was new, I had only seen pictures. The parade was all I hoped it would be and more; it was quite impressive. It actually still is one of my favorite things to see at Disney World. Also, we started to meet friends and site followers that we had previously "met" online. The power of social media really is something; it facilitated the start of our social circle in Florida. When we lived in Michigan, the opportunity rarely presented itself to meet Main Streeters in person. In Florida, though, we were 10 minutes from World Drive, and as people came to town, there was a much greater chance to meet up.

The first couple of times I saw people in the parks with TMSM buttons on, it took me aback a little. To see people who don't even really know us representing our site was very humbling. We saw two when we got our annual passes at Downtown Disney (not yet Disney Springs) and those ladies became good friends of ours. At the Magic Kingdom the day we went to see the parade, we saw a family with buttons on. All I can do when I see that is thank them, give them a hug, and let them know how much it's appreciated. It's a blessing, for sure.

CHAPTER TEN

Adjusting

Remember when I said we were in vacation mode when we first moved? It was starting to catch up with us. We were staying up late, sleeping in, eating dinner later than we normally would, etc. Like vacation. It was fun but exhausting, and I knew we couldn't keep that up forever. Another thing that was an adjustment, that I hadn't thought of ... you can't keep spending money like you're on vacation. When we used to go to Disney for a week, we'd buy fun souvenirs, get the Disney Dining Plan, and eat a ton of food including snacks and desserts, and sometimes do extra activities if we could swing it. The kids would get a Mickey ice cream bar whenever they wanted one. You get the idea.

Well, not anymore. It's a big difference when it all comes out of your pocket. You have to watch what you buy or you can quickly go broke inside a park. We started making adjustments like splitting meals and drinks, bringing granola bars or snacks with us to the parks, and we stopped browsing the gift shops so much to help avoid temptation. It was hard to grasp and separate what was now real life with what used to be vacation. Some things stick out: we never had to cut grass on vacation, or pay bills, or work, or cook dinner. It's all about adjusting and finding a balance. A new normal.

Since we moved away in mid-June, our first holiday in Florida would be the Fourth of July. This might not seem like a big one, but for my family it was. Each year my parents have a big family party on the 4th. To make matters harder, for us, there was a family reunion at my uncle's house around that same time. I knew I'd have to watch for pics on Facebook or hope my dad texted me some pictures. When you dislike change, I suppose it's expected that things will be hard when they're different from what you're used to. For the sake of the kids, and I guess my own sanity, I needed to find a way for us to stay busy over the holiday so that we wouldn't feel as homesick. Lucky for me, Disney throws a great show for the Fourth of July holiday, and I had a plan.

We had never seen the 360-degree fireworks show that Disney puts on for this holiday, so that was on the agenda. We watched the show from inside the Magic Kingdom on July 3, and it was crazy. The fireworks were wonderful, but we encountered our first "holiday" weekend inside a park, and it was crowded beyond belief. We found a spot for the show early, and once the time got closer, you couldn't move. My little guy actually got ran over and stepped on by a rowdy tour group. It was a lesson, for sure. The show itself was unlike anything I'd ever seen. The kids were amazed, too, and it was a relief to see the look on their faces. I was so worried that they'd get homesick or sad, and keeping them busy was a good thing.

The next night, on the actual holiday, we were invited to the Contemporary Resort to watch the fireworks up on the concierge level. One of our sponsors was staying there, so they asked us to bring the boys up for the festivities. We have never stayed at the Contemporary. It's a little too expensive for our budget, so it was exciting to go see how the "other half" lives. The concierge level was beautiful, and was filled with appetizers, drinks, and desserts. The kids couldn't believe that they were just allowed to have snacks and pop (yes, we still call it pop, not soda) whenever they wanted to. Also, there was an amazing view of the Magic Kingdom from the balcony, and when the fireworks started, they piped the music through the speakers to make it that much better. It was beautiful. I had never watched Disney fireworks from a bird's-eye view. We all had a great night and I was thankful for the opportunity.

It was around this time that I started to feel my heart tug a little, because I wished my family and friends back home could see what I was seeing. I wanted them to experience the Disney magic with me, so they would know a little bit of how it feels and why Disney has meant so much to us. One thing at a time, though; I was still getting settled, but in the back of my head, I made a mental note to get as many of them here as possible, eventually. It was a good goal to have.

The next day, Disney launched a new seasonal event at Hollywood Studios: Frozen Summer Fun. This was bad timing for us because we were up extremely late the night before, but it was "work obligation".

A big reason for our moving to Florida was being able to cover events and shows at Disney on our own, without having to rely on other people to get the scoop for us. *Frozen* was still all the rage, and Disney was devoting a full summer in honor of that film, so I knew we needed to go, tired or not. This was the first event we were covering on-site. We had readers at home waiting for us to bring them the details of Frozen Summer Fun, and I didn't want to blow it.

When we got to the park, we checked the times guide and tried to make a plan for the day. I knew I needed to get footage and pictures of everything I could. This was it, this is why we're here! That day was a blur, it was so busy. We covered the Frozen Sing-Along, parade, stage show, and lastly the beautiful Frozen fireworks. While we were there, we got to meet some Main Streeters, plus get a feel of the local blogging community. Before we moved, people warned me that it was going to be hard down here, when it came to others in the industry. Where I came from, we were pretty trusting, so it was hard for me to wrap my head around the advice I had been given. So there we were, standing in a sea of Disney bloggers and media, and I was bound to be cordial and polite, as we were the new kids in town. I felt like we made it, like we belonged. That feeling didn't last, but I'll touch on that a bit more later.

As much as I was having fun in Florida, I was missing home. It had only been about three weeks since I had seen my family and friends, but it felt like a lot longer. You have to make adjustments on so many things when making a big move, and learning to be on your own is one of them. Usually, if we got a little lonely or wanted company, we only had to drive about 10 minutes to get to someone, mostly my parents. Now, we were just keeping busy, and it was working, somewhat. The boys were having a great time, it was like an extended vacation, and I was fine with that. We had a lot of time before school was to start, so I wanted them to enjoy as much of their summer vacation as possible. It's surreal to think that just a few months prior, I was sitting in my freezing cold living room in Michigan, wondering if I could actually make this move, and now we were weeks into it. Time was flying. We went from chilly temps to heat and lots of rain. The summer we moved to Florida, it seemed to rain every single day, and it kept us indoors.

I knew that summertime in Florida is typical for rain showers, but it had been raining much more than I anticipated. Sometimes the rain was so hard that the windows in the house would shake and buckets of rain would fall from the roof. We lost power a few times. Since we were now locals now and could just go back to the parks on another day, we usually decided to stay home on rainy days.

In addition to missing friends and family back home, we were quickly learning that the food down here in Florida is not the same as what we were used to. Two things in particular that we found ourselves missing were pizza and Chinese food. We had tried a few different local pizza places here, but they all were less than good. Back home in Michigan we used to frequent a family-owned restaurant that had the best pizza, and we sure were missing that. Come to find out after speaking with others who moved here from up north, good pizza is hard to find for a lot of people. We really hadn't looked too far to find decent Chinese food; I was almost afraid to look. I suppose that could be filed under foodie problems for those recently relocated to Florida. Ask anyone, the struggle is real! It added to the list of things that I wanted to do once we were able to go back home for visit. Yes, I wanted to see our friends and family, but there are also restaurants that I miss nearly as much. Florida, for example, doesn't have "Coney Island" restaurants. They're low-cost, greasy-spoon type diners popular and prevalent in Michigan. You can get cheap breakfasts, or wait and have chili cheese fries for dinner. Truly the best. We quickly found out that Florida not only doesn't have them, but most people don't even know what they are. Tragic.

As annual passholders, we can visit the parks as often as we like. Sometimes it would rain in the daytime, so we would stay home until evening and then head out to the parks. We went back to see the Frozen fireworks for a leisurely night out instead of covering the show for work. It was nice to be able to have the option to come and go as we please, and not make every outing about the site. We also wanted to do activities that we never had the opportunity to do before. It had been three years since we had a Disney vacation, and so many things had either changed or been added. Out of all the parks, we spent the most time at Magic Kingdom, my favorite park, and with the addition of New Fantasyland, there were extra things that I needed to see. As the mom of two boys, I don't always get to enjoy the "girly stuff," or the princess side of Disney. However, I told the boys that mommy needs to get some material for the site, so we had to go in and actually see some of the attractions that Disney gears toward girls.

First on that list was a new attraction, Enchanted Tales with Belle. I talked the boys into giving it a try. Little did they know, the cast members pick volunteers out of the crowd, and my younger son, Aidan, got chosen to play Belle's father. At the end, he got a bookmark and a photo with Belle, and she called him handsome before we left. That made his night, and it amused his older brother, Andrew.

We were about one month into our new adventures here in Florida, and while we were doing our best to adjust, I also was keeping in mind that I didn't want the kids to lose any of their Disney magic. When we would come here for vacation, the kids were filled with wonder and immersed in the magic that Disney has to offer. Now that we actually lived here, I was a little bit worried that the kids might get tired of going to Disney as often as we did. I know it sounds crazy that a person could get tired of Disney, but I never wanted them to take for granted where we lived now. When we would go to Florida on vacation, they looked forward to seeing characters, parades, fireworks, and other Disney staples. I didn't want those happy feelings to fade. I remember that one of the biggest questions people would ask me once we moved was if I thought I would ever get tired of going to Disney World. People wanted to know if the Disney life would get old after a while. I did wonder about that myself. People dream of moving to their favorite vacation destinations, but not many actually do it, so I was like a case study for those who wanted to follow in our footsteps one day. Some people thought it was a crazy idea, and in some ways it is, but the leap was already taken and I was bound to figure out how to make the best of everything, while educating others in the process.

Sometimes my mind would play tricks on me and I would feel like I was just on a very long vacation. One evening we closed out the Magic Kingdom and didn't get home until about two in the morning. The weather was so humid and hot, even at that time of the evening. We got home and I remember going outside to put my feet in the pool. It was so quiet back there, and I just looked up at the stars, almost having a moment with God, finally realizing that yes we did this and yes we were here. Before I knew it, I was in the water with my clothes still on, just floating in the water, looking up at the sky. A little while later, Scott came outside looking for me, and asked me why I was in the pool with my clothes on at 2 o'clock in the morning. The only answer that came out of my mouth was, "I don't know, maybe because I can?" I think it was sometime that evening that I finally made peace with the fact that we were down here for at least a year to come, the lease was signed and there was no going back, and this was now home. It's funny how you go through phases when you are pushing yourself out of your own comfort zone. All those years that I said I wanted to move to Florida, all the plans I made that never came to be, I actually did it this time, and I still couldn't figure out how I got up the nerve to do it. I'm a work in progress, at least that's what I tell people when I don't have all the answers.

CHAPTER ELEVEN

Meet-up Time and More Adjusting

Around the same time, in the midst of adjusting to our new lives, I wanted to push forward and do one of the things that I only had dreamed about doing: have a Main Street Mouse meet up! Since we started the site four years prior, it had always been a hope of mine to meet some of the people who stood by what we do and help make TMSM a happy place. It's funny because up until this point I had never even met in person the people who work with us, and I wanted to change that as well.

One of my admins, Autumn, was going to be in town for the week, so not only did I want to finally meet her in person, we also decided to put together a quick meet up at Epcot. Since that we didn't give people much notice, I wasn't sure what to expect when we put out the information that we were going to be at Epcot that Wednesday evening to meet some of our readers and watch the fireworks together.

When we arrived at Epcot, the plan was to meet a few people at Electric Umbrella to eat, then head over to World Showcase to meet the rest of the group. We found more Main Streeters at the electric umbrella than we expected, and our dinner group got even bigger. Before we knew it, it was time for us to walk over to World Showcase, where the actual meet-up was to begin. I was nervous and didn't know what to expect. I had all of these thoughts running through my head; the biggest one was wondering if anyone would actually show up. As we approached the meet-up location, I saw a lot of people there waiting for us. I was in disbelief that so many came out on short notice, but then I began to worry that I couldn't pull off a successful gathering with that large of a group. Self-doubt is a horrible thing, but it sure does get the best of us sometimes. We started walking around greeting everyone who was there, and I think I gave each person a hug because I was so thankful and humbled that people actually took time out of their evening to come out and meet us. I had a cast member friend named Chuck, who took photos for Disney, so we put him in charge of gathering the group together for our first meet-up photo. There were so many people there, he had to keep backing up to fit everyone in the shot. It was truly overwhelming.

After we took the group photo, even more people showed up and truly my heart was full. So, yes, there were a lot of people there, my fear of no one showing was unwarranted ... now what? We decided to take the group for a walk around World Showcase. Some folks wanted to grab a drink, some wanted a bite to eat, and others were just looking for a spot from where our group could watch the night-time show, IllumiNations, together. We ended up in the back of the park and continued the Main Streeter party, waiting for the show to begin. Everyone seemed to be having a good time, and I was, too.

When IllumiNations ended, most people stuck around to chat even more. We gradually made our way to the front of the park, and began to say our goodbyes. There were a handful of us that hung back, to recap the evening and give our thoughts on how things went. All in all, everyone agreed that our first meet-up was a complete success. All that worrying I did was for nothing, because things went better than I could have imagined. Both Autumn and my friend Lorraine chipped in and bought me a Disney bracelet, sort of as a congratula-tory gift, and I finally lost it. It was the cherry on the Disney sundae. Just like I couldn't believe we actually moved, I couldn't believe that so many people cared this much about The Main Street Mouse and the efforts we make to provide a safe and fun Disney community. Talk about humbling. Chuck looked at me and said, "You have something special here, kid." He was right, I did. Now I knew we had more work to do, and this was just the beginning.

It was nice having Autumn in town, and making new friends at the meet-up, but I still was on the lookout for places or activities to do that reminded me of home. For instance, twice a year in Michigan, we would visit a little town called Frankenmuth, where they have Bronners, the world's biggest year-round Christmas store. So, as a substitute, we'd browse the Christmas store at Magic Kingdom.

Not the same, I know, but good enough for the time being. You'd be surprised what you'll find comforting when you have little to work with. Plus, my kids say the Christmas store smells like Grandma's house at the holidays. It's a win-win!

You can't make too many comparisons when it comes to Michigan versus Florida. One thing Florida has that Michigan surely doesn't? Bugs. Big bugs. People told me about the possibility of seeing some creepy crawlies once we moved here, but to actually witness them is a huge difference.

The horror stories are true. Florida has big hairy spiders call wolf spiders, but thankfully we've only seen them dead, as we constantly spray bug killer all around the house. The biggest offender we had heard about are the dreaded Palmetto bugs, or as I call them, big nasty cockroaches. Palmetto bug sounds so much nicer, doesn't it? I had a friend when I moved here who had an obsessive fear of Palmetto bugs, which worked in my favor because he'd tell me where to find them and how to avoid them. That was excellent information to know, especially since my boys had never seen anything like them.

One place you want to avoid, if you're not fond of big nasty cockroaches, is Adventureland at the Magic Kingdom. Apparently, Palmetto bugs take a liking to the drips coming off of Dole Whips and Citrus Swirls, plus there are a lot of bushes and plants for them to hide in. Late one evening we went to Adventureland to grab a last-minute Citrus Swirl before leaving the park. We got our ice cream and began walking. My younger son went to sit down, and out of the corner of my eye, I saw something move. Something much bigger than just a normal, run-of-the-mill bug. There is it was, in all its glory, the Palmetto bug. I screamed, then Aidan screamed, and my friend laughed and said, "I told you so!" To this day, I won't sit anywhere near plants in Adventureland at night. I can laugh about it now. We never had bugs big enough to put a saddle on back home, but down here, it's a whole new way of life. Other favored locales for Palmetto bugs at Magic Kingdom are the Swiss Family Treehouse and Tom Sawyer Island. Snakes, too. Did I mention snakes?

CHAPTER TWELVE

Making the Most of Summer

The first Florida summer was cruising right along. We were looking at the end of July already, and I knew it wouldn't be long before the fun was over and the kids had to go back to school. New schools. I was a nervous mess. The thought of sending them to school, where they knew no one, really tore me up. When I was a kid, we stayed in the same school district the entire time, so I didn't know what it was like to have to go through changes like that. I wasn't ready to think about it yet, so I wanted to make the most of our last few weeks of freedom before the daily grind of school pick ups and homework began.

As it was such a rainy summer, there were certain things we didn't get to spend a lot of time exploring, like Epcot, for one. Test Track had gotten a make-over before we moved, and we hadn't been on it yet. We finally took the kids on the all-new Test Track, and they loved it; not surpsingly, since they've always loved cars. I think I had more Matchbox cars in my house than anyone else. In Test Track, they got to make their own cars on the computer, then do more activities after the ride. Also, we did the KidCot activity in World Showcase, where kids can get their name written in the language of every pavilion country. We hadn't done that before, either. We also tried the fan-favorite "cronut" at the Canada pavilion.

Even though we were cramming in our last bits of summer fun, I was still watching the weather and happenings back home in Michigan. Thank God for social media; it makes it really easy to keep up on things. During that time, the folks back home were experiencing unusually cold weather, while we were here dying in the heat.

A little break would have been nice, but maybe not as chilly as they were having it. The end of the summer in Michigan is always nice, though. The evenings were getting cooler, and summer festivals were still going on. The city I lived in, Allen Park, had their annual street fair each year in August. It's my favorite. Actually, the last few years we were there, we worked the street fair at a booth, selling our crafts. In Michigan, street fairs are hugely popular. There are the summer fairs, followed closely by the fall fairs. We don't have those types of things in Florida, so I had to watch friends and family posting pics on Facebook. Good news came when my parents called and told me they had booked a trip to come and see us in mid September. It gave us all something to look forward to. I knew that we had a lot that we were working on and that time would pass quickly. A plan needed to be made, of course; just one more thing to work on!

We were now in our seventh week as Floridians. I wanted to make the most of what we had left of the craziest summer we've ever had. It's funny how when you are a vacationer and visit Walt Disney World, sometimes you keep to the same routines. Same resorts, same attractions, same restaurants. We were that way. Whenever we'd plan a Disney trip, we'd find ourselves being creatures of habit, and we'd make reservations at restaurants that we've eaten at before, or stayed in places that were comfortable and familiar. There's nothing wrong with that, of course. Once we moved to the Orlando area, I realized how many things at Disney World that we did *not* do before.

One evening, based on someone's recommendation, we went over to Fort Wilderness and had dinner at their buffet restaurant, Trail's End. Oddly, I never even known about Trail's End. We'd been to Fort Wilderness only once, and that was to go to Mickey's Backyard BBQ. It rained like cats and dogs that night, so we were running from place to place, without much opportunity to sight-see. By the time we got back to the pavilion for the Backyard BBQ, we were soaked down to the skin, I had ruined an expensive pair of shoes, and we focused on making the most of the experience, even wet and cold.

This time, however, we took the boat ride from the Magic Kingdom to Fort Wilderness, I had never done that before. The first thing I noticed once we got going was the trees around the lake past the Contemporary Resort. It reminded me of home when we'd vacation "up north," as Michiganders call it. It still does remind me of home when we go on the boat, but I think back then, it meant even more.

I was looking around, trying to find some comfort and familiarity, even among the palm trees and hot temperatures. Once we got to the dock, we walked around the grounds a little bit before dinner.

Trail's End has a great buffet. I was talking to our server, and she said not a lot of people even realize that they're there, so they usually aren't too busy. Another reason she gave for the low crowds was the fact that there's no straight shot to their establishment. People either need to take the boat over, or drive to the campground parking lot and take a bus; you can't simply park at the restaurant and walk in.

So, dinner was good, and afterwards we did some more exploring. The horse stables are right next door, and if you keep going, you'll find the walking/bike trails. Even though we didn't know where the trails led, we decided to follow them. The trails are beautiful, with wispy trees and flowers. It felt like home, too. Also, I didn't realize that there were many deer on the premises, which was awesome to see. Even though we were on Disney property, it sure didn't feel that way. Disney has a way of making you forget other places when you're at any location, and truly, it was hard to imagine that just a short distance away there were rides, fireworks, and parades. Fort Wilderness is an escape from the Disney hustle and bustle, and it's a good thing. We ended up at the Wilderness Lodge, another place I had never been to. We explored the resort, and eventually ended up back at the Magic Kingdom later that evening.

Another first, and this was pretty amazing, was closing the Magic Kingdom. A lot of people do that now, but a couple of years ago, it wasn't as popular. I hadn't done it yet. One Friday evening, (this is a good tip: wait until the sun is lower, then go to the parks, it's not as hot!) we had FastPasses for the Magic Kingdom. We did some character meet and greets, watched the later run of the Main Street Electrical Parade, and stood in line for the Seven Dwarfs Mine Train. Once all those activities were done, it was late, really late, and the park was closed. I don't believe we've ever stayed in a Disney park so late before. When we got off Mine Train, we started walking toward the carousel, and to my surprise, the area around it was empty. There was no one back there, just cast members. It was so odd to see the park mostly devoid of guests. The good thing, was that this is a great opportunity to take some amazing photos of some of your favorite Disney things, minus the crowds. I felt like a kid in a candy store. We took photos of the carousel, the back of Cinderella Castle, and parts of Fantasyland, and were the only ones there. It was surreal ... but it got even better.

I talked to a cast member, just to make sure it was alright that we were there, and he said to go ahead and walk through the castle, which I did. Once I got through the castle, the view was breathtaking. It's not often that you get to enjoy the streets of the Magic Kingdom alone. Granted, it was around one o'clock in the morning, but staying up late was worth it. I felt like a little kid again. I was probably more excited to be there that late than my boys were. They didn't appreciate it like I did. As I stood there, at the door of Cinderella Castle, I felt like a princess. Yes, as cliche as it sounds, I felt like a princess and the castle felt like home. It's hard to explain without sounding completely cheesy, but I promise, it's an overwhelming and magical feeling. All that dreaming, all those years of only wishing I could be there and do things like that ... and there I was. The cast member could see my eyes welling up with tears, and he told me to take my time and let me know when he wanted me to close "my door" for the night. My door? Okay, tears really flowed. God bless him for being so nice. I wanted him to be able to go home so I told him go ahead and close it.

After walking off "my porch" at the castle, I went down by the *Partners* statue to get a few more pictures. Just then, I heard the sprinkling of pixie dust, and the "Kiss Goodnight" began. Another first for me. There was no one there but us, yet this awesome production was playing, so of course I had to grab my tablet and record it. It felt like a dream. My heart was just swelling with emotion, and I was trying to not shake while recording the castle lights. Although I didn't want to leave, out of respect for the cast members, we headed for the front of the park. It's an experience I'll never forget, and something I knew I wanted to do again.

If you've never stayed until the park closes, grab yourself some caffeine and hang around until after hours. It was that little bit of extra magic I needed to help close out the summer.

CHAPTER THIRTEEN

Here Comes Reality

Even among the magic and last-minute summer activities, it wasn't all fun. Reality was creeping in, and fun had to take a backseat to things that needed to be done. We had preparations to make, as the kids were getting ready to start at their new school. It was a K-8 school, so the boys got to start off together, which was a comfort. The schools are different down here. I was still on Michigan time, where schools start after Labor Day. Not here. School begins in August, so time was running out. Kids have to get physicals before they're allowed to enroll, so we had to find a clinic to have that done. Not only was it expensive, but it was inconvenient, as we had to wait quite awhile in the lobby for a quick check up. Everyone in town must have decided to go to the same place we did. The kids weren't happy, neither was I, but you do what you have to do. Speaking of unhappy, another switch from Michigan to Florida: the schools here have a dress code. My boys had a lot of clothes, and unfortunately, they couldn't wear most of it to school. I needed to find plain polo shirts in either white, navy, or burgundy. Easy, right? No. Every place we looked, they were out of the colors we needed, so finding plain shirts became a scavenger hunt. We were running out of time, and they had nothing to wear to school. It figures.

In the meantime, I took the boys to the open house to get their schedules and let them walk around to find where their classes were. The layout for schools here in Florida is so very different than what we were used to. The campus is open, kids walk outside from building to building, they have areas where the classrooms are clustered into "pods," or in layman terms, big trailers. I'm not sure who was more nervous, me or them. Okay, it was me. The self-doubt was high that day. What did I do? This school is huge.

In addition to class schedules, we got the supply list for the year. Oh. My. Gosh. Not only did I have to spring for a physical and specific clothing, here comes the supply list. It was huge. We headed to Walmart to get some items on the list, and it looked like the health clinic: everyone in town was there fighting for the right color folders and number two pencils. Insanity. They even print out school lists at the front of the store, which I had never seen before, so you'd know what supplies to get. People say that the cost of living is cheaper in the south, but not here, not near the theme parks. We had to get school essentials, plus take care of daily expenses and bills, and it felt like we were drowning. There was a point where we were looking for items to sell that we brought from home that we didn't really need, as there are a lot of pawn shops down here. I also began rummaging through some of my jewelry to sell, as there are also places who buy gold all over town. Somehow, we made it through.

Even with all the stress, I didn't want to let on that I was worried where the kids were concerned. It was the last weekend before school and I wanted to let them have a pinch more fun before the daily grind began. We did something we hadn't done, and which costs nothing ... visit the beach! We had been in Florida for two months and I still hadn't been to the shore, so I looked online to see which beaches were the closest to home. Cocoa Beach was it, so that's where we headed.

As we drove, we approached Port Canaveral, and saw some of the enormous cruise ships that were docked, including one from the Disney Cruise Line. It was exciting, as we'd never been there before. We found a place to park near Ron Jon's Surf Shop, then walked down to the beach. The ocean air was so welcoming. It was hot outside, but the breeze made a huge difference. In Michigan, we're used to the lakes, but the ocean is on such a bigger scale that the boys were a little nervous to go in. As we were finding a spot, a man asked Aidan, "Did you know that it's shark week?" and he was about done before we even started. So, to ease their minds a little, I got in the water with them, and told them to not go too deep. We ended up sitting on the shore, playing in the waves, and had a wonderful time. After all was said and done, I think between all of us we had enough sand in our bathing suits to build a sandcastle, but it was worth it. Being away from everything and everyone was nice. No crowds, no noise, no worries.

I didn't want to leave the beach, for I knew that the next day our summer fun was over, and it was time to get down to real life here in Florida. I reflected a bit on the summer and all that we had been through. So many ups and downs, and yet we haven't packed it all in yet and headed back north. Failure wasn't an option at that point, I didn't care what we had to do. We needed to give this new life a fair chance.

As we packed up our beach toys and towels, the boys were a little sad, as they didn't want to go back home yet. My only regret was not going to the beach sooner, as it was a good escape. When we got back to the house, it was time to get their backpacks together, lay out their school clothes, and get them showered and ready for morning. They weren't scared, but I was. The thought of them having a bad day or them hating their school weighed heavy on my heart. The fresh beach air made them tired, so they didn't even fight me about going to bed a little earlier.

The next morning I got up, made them breakfast, got them in their school uniforms, and took those traditional first-day-of-school pictures. Each year I make them humor me, and have them sit still for two minutes for back-to-school photos. This year, however, they stood on our patio, with a palm tree in the background. It was a different look. When we got to the school, the drop-off line was so long I thought that they would be late for class because it took forever to get to the door. We finally got up to the drop-off point. I told them I loved them and wished them good luck on their first day. What came next? You guessed it, tears, but not until I had driven away. You know how you see those commercials of parents dancing and singing about how happy they are that school is starting? I'm the opposite. I'd rather have the boys home with me. People had mentioned that home schooling is big here in Florida, and I thought about that for a minute or two, but the kids wanted to make new friends and give the school a chance, and I think that was best, too. Letting go is hard, but on this journey it's been a necessity. I was getting better at it, slowly but surely.

Lo and behold, the pick-up line at the end of the day was even worse that the drop-off line that morning. Another little bit of something new to adjust to. The kids got in the car, all smiles. They had a good day, thank God. Saying I was relieved is an understatement. Their school year started off on the right foot, and I was thankful.

At this point, the kids were settling in with their new school and schedule, and we, too, were adjusting to a new routine. Fun time was about done, the day-to-day of "real" life came first. People who have lived here for a while said that the rain over that summer was the most they'd seen in years. It rained every day, it seemed, and not just a quick shower, it was more like half-day downpours. We were working, the kids were in school, but it rained and rained. That being said, I was hopeful to do another TMSM mini meet-up, despite the iffy weather.

At the end of August, we did a meet-up at Hollywood Studios to catch those beautiful Frozen fireworks before they were gone. That day at home was a hard one. I had gotten my first dose of how harsh the Disney community can be down here, and I wasn't handling it well. Some online bullying was going on, and truthfully, I wasn't ready for it. Granted, it happened here and there when we first started out, but not since we moved. Some of the people I had met and hoped would be friends of ours actually weren't friends. As the new kids in town, we were looked upon as competition, and I quickly started to learn where I stood. Our meet up was that evening, and I didn't even want to go. Not because I didn't want to see some of our members, but because my spirit was just broken, and to me, staying home where I felt "safe" was easier. Did I stay home? Nope, sure didn't. Why? I don't know. That same mental kick in the pants that made me have the guts to move here creeped back up and told me to get myself to Hollywood Studios. I forced myself to get motivated and headed out.

By the time we got to Hollywood Studios, storm clouds were rolling in. Of course they were! We made it to the back of the park and ducked out from the rain at the Backlot Express. Some of our group was there, so we hunkered down together. As we sat and visited, I was getting messages from others, saying that the weather was too bad and they weren't able to make it. One family messaged me from the parking lot to let me know they were turning around and going home due to the storm. My day wasn't going well.

The rain eventually ended, and we started to walk to the spot where we said for folks to meet us. Even though the park was filled with puddles and a lot of people went home, as we walked up, there they were. People standing around, wearing TMSM buttons, waiting for our group. That's what it's all about. Those people are the reason I do what I do. The weather was bad, my outlook on things here was worse, but yet I got the much-needed reminder that people do care. Do you let others bring you down, or do you keep fighting to do whatever you can to overcome? Keep fighting. Overcome. It's not easy to do, but I knew I had to try. That night I saw some familiar faces, people who were at the first meet-up, and that was a welcome sight. Some of these people were locals, like my cast member friend Chuck and the girls I labeled the TMSM super fans, Janet and Cindy. All were there, plus some new faces. We talked, listened to some music courtesy of "DJ Chill," and watched the gorgeous fireworks. Afterward, some people stuck around to chat about future meet-ups. Our first big annual event was coming in October, and they were all willing to pitch in and help with whatever we needed.

Sometimes we get prayers answered, even when we don't specifically ask. If I would have let people get the best of me, and cancelled the meet up, then I wouldn't have gotten the boost that I needed. Sure, not everyone who is nice to your face really has your best interest at heart, but that doesn't mean that you close yourself off to everyone out of fear. I'm glad I didn't do that, even though I was ready to. I'll never forget that night and how much those nice people lifted my spirits at the right time. So, afterward, I knew I needed to press on, as there was so much more to do.

CHAPTER FOURTEEN

Fall and Family

Before we knew it, September was here. In what seemed like overnight, Disney's Magic Kingdom had gone through a complete Halloween makeover. We knew it was coming because of the merchandise in the stores and the Halloween windows on Main Street, U.S.A. I hadn't seen the fall decorations in three years at that point, and I had forgotten how much I missed it all. Hints of orange were sprinkled throughout the streets when you walked into the park, Mickey Mouse pumpkin wreaths were all on all of the light posts, carved pumpkins were settled above doorways and on top of buildings ... and it was beautiful. I kept saying how I'd love to have one of those Mickey wreaths for the front door of my home. I'm sure a lot of you would, too! Mickey's Not So Scary Halloween Party, a separate ticket event, was kicking off as well, but we didn't attend. Now that we were locals, we had to pick and choose what extra activities we did, and when. We knew we couldn't afford to go multiple times, so we had to choose our date wisely for the halloween party. Not to mention, I needed time to get costumes together for our family, or at least Halloween shirts. The kids really wanted to go, but I told them that we needed to wait a little while. It's not vacation anymore, real life had set in; we had priorities and other things that needed to come first, but I wasn't complaining.

The kids were well settled into their school routines at this point. I was seeing friends in Michigan posting their back-to-school pics online, and we had already been at it for a few weeks. Labor Day came, and instead of going to a BBQ at my parents house like usual, we went to Hollywood Studios. We were just biding our time, because in a couple of weeks my parents would be here for a visit. Meanwhile, we started to do some more exploring—when it wasn't raining, that is. Most of the summer, we spent time at Hollywood Studios or Magic

Kingdom. When fall hit, we found ourselves frequenting Epcot. Their yearly food and wine festival was starting, and we were excited to check things out since we had never gone before. Also, I was finding a new appreciation for World Showcase. There is a lot more to do there than meets the eye. When we were just vacationing, we'd get through World Showcase pretty quickly, as we were on limited time, and, of course, the kids would pick rides over strolling around. Getting the kids interested in that section of Epcot was easier than I thought, especially with the KidCot activity and collecting stamps in each country. It was a whole new world for them, and they enjoyed it.

Finally, it was almost time for my parents to visit. I hadn't seen them in three months, and that was the longest amount of time we'd ever gone without seeing each other. They were going to spend a week here, and gave me the green light to play tour guide and show them around, which I was excited about doing. My father hadn't been to Disney World in over 20 years (remember that whole "mouse park" thing)? I so badly wanted to change his mind about Disney. For my mother, it had been about 11 years since she'd been to Disney, so she was a bit more familiar. There was so much that we wanted to show them, and a limited time in which to do it. The kids kept singing "I can show you the world" every time we mentioned the grandparents coming to visit. They were looking forward to it as well.

My parents love Florida, but the easy-going aspect of it, like going out to eat and visiting the beach, so I had to factor that in. If I could only choose one park to take them, however, it would be my favorite, Magic Kingdom. They would be surprised at how much things had changed over the years, but still get to enjoy some classic attractions like the Haunted Mansion. Playing tour guide was a challenge I was up for, but truly, I was just looking forward to having family here.

While waiting on my parents' visit, the husband and I were trying to do more Disney things that we'd never done, and one day while the kids were in schoolwe went to Animal Kingdom to check out Rafiki's Planet Watch. Can you believe I had never done that before? We also stood in line for the Dug and Russel from *UP* meet and greet. These are what I now call "work trips." We live close to Disney, but Disney is also my job, and the site our bread and butter. We have to stay current on what's going on in the parks, by taking pictures and video. Not to mention, I need to have material to write about. Before we moved, I was at a huge disadvantage when it came to topics. I'd go to the Disney Store when I was desperate for inspiration. That wasn't a problem here. Part of my job running TMSM is to bring the Disney magic to people from everywhere, all walks of life, even when they can't physically be at the parks. I was also finding that we had a decent size following in the UK, Australia, and Brazil. In addition to reporting, I was also taking time to do a "Random Acts of Disney Kindness" blog to give extra credit to cast members who go out of their way to make sure guests have a magical time.

The Wednesday night my parents arrived in town, the kids and I were looking out the front windows at home, waiting for their rental car to pull up in the driveway. It felt like waiting for Santa on Christmas Eve. When they finally got here, we all ran outside to greet them. After some hugs and tears, we came inside, as I had made them some Italian food for dinner. We ate and visited. It was long overdue. The next day, the kids had school, but Scott and I took my parents to Downtown Disney for lunch at Earl of Sandwich, a new experience for them. They liked looking around, and my dad really liked the Earl's Holiday Turkey Sandwich. My job as tour guide had begun.

Friday night, I had it all planned out. We were going to go over to the Magic Kingdom, take the boat to Fort Wilderness, and have dinner at Trail's End. Since we enjoyed their buffet so much, I thought my parents might like it, too, plus they could see the sights as well. It didn't go as well as I had hoped. It started to rain, and rain ... and rain. When we got to the Transportation and Ticket Center, they had closed the monorail due to the rain, so we had to take the ferryboat over. Once we got to the front of the Magic Kingdom and to the proper boat dock, we found that they were only using one boat for multiple stops, and we had to stand in the rain and wait. By the time we finally got to Trail's End, we were soaked, cold, and over an hour late for our dinner reservation. So much for me changing my dad's opinion about Disney and what it has to offer. At this point, I was in the negative, even though it was beyond my control. The bright side was that my parents loved the restaurant, so I was back on the scoreboard.

Afterward, we took the boat back to the main gate. HalloWishes, the Halloween fireworks from Mickey's Not So Scary Halloween Party, were just starting. We got to hear the show and see the tops of the fireworks. My dad cracked his rough anti-Disney exterior when he saw the fireworks. His face lit up like a kid, and honestly that did my heart good. My mom loved it, too. I so badly wanted them to have a good time, and for them to see why my love for Disney turned into this crazy whirlwind of a job that I have.

The next day, to no one's surprise, it was raining. It was decision time on what we were going to do, and we opted to go to the Magic Kingdom regardless of weather and pray for the best. I had a whole day planned out, and was hoping that things wouldn't get rained out like they did the night before. A few items were on my must-do list for the day. This was my shot to convert my dad. For one, I felt they needed to see the Festival of Fantasy Parade. We found a spot in the hub, near Walt and Mickey, and grabbed a bench to wait. My mom was having headaches, which at this point we weren't sure as to why, so I wanted to find a spot where they both could rest while waiting. When the parade came they both stood up to watch. To my surprise and absolute delight, I looked over at my dad and he was recording the parade on his phone, with a smile on his face. Another point for me!

Another item on the list: classic attractions. We took them on the Haunted Mansion and Pirates of the Caribbean. My dad was impressed with the queue lines for these rides, and all the details that Disney puts into what they do. So far, so good. Before the night was out, we saw the Main Street Electrical Parade, which they both enjoyed. And finally: Wishes. Seeing the look on my parents faces was worth it all. Mission accomplished.

It's funny how, as we get older, the dynamics change between parents and children. They used to worry about me, whether I was taken care of, or having a good time. This time it was me, wanting more than anything to bring that Disney joy to them, to make sure they had a good time ... and they did. The quest to convert them to Mickey fans was working. When my parents first bought tickets, they thought it was a steep price for one day at a theme park. By the time we left, they were saying how great the day was and that it was worth the price of admission.

We only did one park visit. There was just a couple days left in their vacation. A beach day was mentioned, so we drove out to New Smyrna Beach, at the suggestion of a cast member. We had never been there before, and it was an adventure. What's ironic is that after we got home, the news reported that there was an incident at New Smyrna Beach, where someone got bit by a shark, about an hour before we got there. Crazy to think that happened, but in a way I'm glad we didn't know ahead of time, or we might not have enjoyed ourselves.

Before my parents went home, we took them to Downtown Disney (now Disney Springs) one more time, then they cooked dinner for us the night before it was time to head back to Michigan. We cried before they headed out, but I knew that we'd be going home at Christmas time, so I tried to keep them in mind.

Our first fall in Florida pressed on, and changes were happening at Disney World. We knew that Hollywood Studios was in for some switch ups, but were uncertain at that point what it was going to be. Their long-running Backlot Tour was scheduled to be closing for good, so we wanted to go over there and ride it one more time. It's funny how that attraction never had a long line until it was announced that it was soon going to be shut down permanently. The last day of the Backlot Tour, the crowds were pretty high. It's not something that we regularly did, but I knew we needed to go report from the scene and take one last ride. Also closing soon was Maelstrom, the ride located in Epcot's Norway pavilion. There was much more fuss from guests about Maelstrom closing than there was about the Backlot Tour. Even one of my staffers, Corey, was up in arms that Disney was closing his favorite ride. To add insult to injury, not only was Maelstrom closing, Disney was replacing it with a *Frozen*-themed attraction.

Sometimes when we make announcements like this on TMSM, we get a lot of flack and complaints from readers, even though we are just the messenger, not the ones making those decisions. So, just like with the Backlot Tour, we went to Epcot on the last night of Maelstrom for one last ride. We actually did a video, as it was insanely busy. So many people came out to pay their respects to this beloved ride. It's things like this that we couldn't do from home in Michigan. I'd have to do second-hand reporting, which I hated to do. Now, we were able to be on the scene for newsworthy events at Disney, and it was exciting to do. In some respects, Disney fans are like how I am with change ... we don't like it. But where Disney is concerned, Walt himself said that things will always change and move forward, and that is what was happening. We just have to roll with it.

Speaking of change, my kids were doing so much better with it than I was. They were loving their time in Florida, and that was a huge load off my mind. Maybe they're not like me ... they seem to be fine with change. They weren't sad when the Backlot Tour or Maelstrom closed, either. Good for them.

CHAPTER FIFTEEN

Expanding Our Horizons

In addition to our busy Disney schedules, we were branching out to cover more Orlando-area attractions. We created "Off TMSM" which dealt with places like Universal Studios, Sea World, Busch Gardens, and Gatorland. It was adding even more to our plates, but we figured since we're down here, we might as well get as much info out to our readers as we can.

I noticed a big change in myself. I was becoming a workaholic. The more work we did, the more I wanted to do. It was hard to turn that off, even at night when I should be winding down. Our first media event for Off TMSM was for the Halloween festivities at Sea World Orlando. We were so excited that we were invited out to cover their opening day, but a little nervous, too. This was outside of our Disney bubble, a bit out of our comfort zone. The kids were excited, as we'd never been to Sea World, so we went to the media event. We got to do some trick-or-treating, see a few shows, and ride some coasters. I know Sea World gets a bad rap in the press sometimes, but it's a great park, and their media department has been lovely to us since we moved here. I felt like we were breaking new ground by covering non-Disney-related events. Some people want to know what else there is to see and do when they visit Orlando, and now I'd be able to tell them about things firsthand. When you run your own ship, you have to read your audience, listen to their questions and interests, and try to bring them what they're looking for. That was the goal with Off TMSM.

Back on the Disney front, things were moving right along. We went to some of the Eat to the Beat concerts at Epcot, as we hadn't done that before. The concerts were fun, and free, so that's even better. Another new idea that came to me once we moved is my "Don't Be That Guy at Disney" blog series. People watching is a favorite activity for so many at Disney, myself included, so I thought I'd do something that's an extention of that. People get offended easily if you're not careful, so although doing a series that included humor and a bit of snark was risky, I wanted to do it the right way. The first blog for series was "Don't Be That Guy at Mickey's PhilharMagic." It was a snarky spin on park etiquette.

To my delight, people loved the new series. No one got mad at me, which was shocking. Actually, people started commenting about different instances where they also saw "that guy" and were writing in about it. Sometimes we have to try a new approach, whether it sticks or not is unknown, but it doesn't hurt to give it a shot. Keeping things fresh is important.

CHAPTER SIXTEEN

Meeting Our Disney Ohana

Our first big TMSM meet-up was almost here. We had smaller get togethers, but this is the one that the most people were coming to, so we had a lot to prepare for. The guest list was getting bigger and bigger as it got closer, and I was getting a bit nervous. My parents had been gone for a few weeks at this point, but I was excited that another part of home was coming to visit. My two best girlfriends from home, Paula and Michelle, were flying in for the big day. I was so looking forward to having them here, as were the boys. They knew having their aunties stay in the house with us meant extra love and spoiling. Being that this was our first big event, it was a comfort to know that my closest friends would be by my side to help. Also coming to the meet up were three of our original members who became staff, Autumn, Corey, and Mike. The three of them had been with us since TMSM was first started, so having them all there was the perfect way to kick off what I hoped to be the first of many annual events.

Preparing for these gatherings is exciting, but also overwhelming. There was a time that I'd only dream of having something like this, where our staff and readers could actually spend park time together, and now it was happening. I wanted to give out prizes as thank-you gifts, so there was that to get ready. We had a bigger prize for those who showed their "TMSM Pride" by making signs, shirts, etc. My hope was that enough people would show up, to where we'd be able to give prizes and justify the cost of doing all of this. I'm used to planning birthday parties for the kids, or holiday BBQ's at home, never anything of this size, and I was scared. Self doubt ... here we go again.

Meet-up weekend was upon us and I was a bundle of nerves. My Michigan sisters were here staying with me, we had lots of Disney friends coming to town, and quite a few Main Streeters that I'd never met before who were planning on being at Epcot that Saturday. The event was a huge success. We had roughly one hundred people, give or take, show up that day, and it was the best feeling. Getting to meet people who have become extended Disney family was a wonderful thing. We met for lunch at the Electric Umbrella, then headed over to Soarin' where more people were waiting. After that, we pulled some strings to do a private character meet-and-greet with Mickey, Minnie, and Goofy. I wish the entire group would have been there for that, as it was true Disney magic. Some went ahead, some went to World Showcase, but the group that got to go in with the characters had a great experience. For my friend Michelle, this was her first time ever visiting Disney, and I wanted to make it extra special for her. While waiting for the characters, we let her go to the front of the line and walk in before the group, so she could have her moment with her first encounter meeting Mickey Mouse. Her mom had recently passed away, and Disney was something that they used to dream about visiting. When she saw Mickey she cried, and he hugged her and gave her extra attention.

Another great thing about the day was having all of our TMSM mods together for the first time. We had worked together for over four years, but we have never all been at the same place at the same time. Getting to thank and hug Autumn, Corey, and Mike was a great feeling. I'm forever grateful to them for believing in me, even at times when I didn't believe in myself. Plus, it was good for our members to get to meet the staff, too.

Another person I got to meet that day was one of our long-time members, Fran. When we met, she hugged me and cried. I never understood until that point how much TMSM meant to her. She said that our site came across at a time in her life when she needed it the most. We gave her a good distraction and a sense of belonging; an extended family. To this day it's hard for me to fully understand the impact TMSM has had on people. The friendships we've formed, the safe place for Disney fans to come together, it's been a blessing.

Later in the day, we met near the area just past Future World for the group picture. There were so many of us that the person taking the photo had to keep moving backwards to fit our entire group into the frame. After the photo, I walked through the crowd, talking to people, thanking them for their support, and also checking out the various TMSM swag that they were representing. People made signs, shirts, TMSM mouse ears, and one of our "super fans" even made a TMSM cape and matching tutu. I was worried that I'd have extra prizes to take home, due to no one participating, but I ended up giving everything I brought away. I felt like Oprah: "You get a prize, and you get a prize...." We spent the rest of the night walking around World Showcase and closed the day out by watching IllumiNations back near the Japan pavilion.

The day after the meet up, we were exhausted, but with Paula and Michelle still in town, we needed to make a plan for more Disney fun. October was almost over, and we still hadn't attended Mickey's Not So Scary Halloween Party. That evening, we all attended the party and had a great time. The Boo to You Parade was spook-tacular, to say the least. And those fireworks that we watched from outside the gates, HalloWishes, were even better than I anticipated, standing front and center at Cinderella Castle.

Halloween finally came, but with no trick or treating with my parents, as usual. I remember sitting in the pick-up line at school and I called them. Traditions are hard to break, but sometimes we have no choice in the matter. They missed us, too, but told me not to be upset, as it was forty degrees and rainy there, so Halloween wasn't going to be too eventful. Friends of ours invited us to come to their house for the evening so the kids could go out for candy together. All in all, it was a pretty good first Halloween in Florida. What I didn't realize fully was that Disney is pretty quick to switch from holiday to holiday, and within a few days, Disney World would be filled with Christmas cheer.

CHAPTER SEVENTEEN

Christmas Cheer

Seemingly overnight, Disney goes from Halloween to Christmas. The Halloween decorations get put away quickly, and there are Christmas wreaths where the pumpkins used to be. In all the years of us going to Disney World, we had never seen it at Christmas time. I had seen pictures and videos, but seeing the festivities in person was something we all were looking forward to.

Word got around that the first lighting of Cinderella Castle was to be taking place, but this year it was the Frozen characters doing the honors, much to the dismay of many die-hard Disney fans. They wanted the Fairy Godmother to resume her role, but that wasn't happening. For me, I didn't really care *who* lit the Castle, I was just excited to finally see it.

The opening of the Christmas season at the Magic Kingdom was of course on a school night, so we had to head right over after picking up the boys, to secure a spot. Every blogger and media outlet in town was there, so I knew we had to grab the best spot possible and stay put until it was showtime. We were not only taking pictures for the site, but also getting video for our YouTube channel so we could share the magic with our followers. So there we were, waiting for the first show of A Frozen Holiday Wish. My stomach was in knots a bit because I was so excited to see my favorite castle all decked out for Christmas. Disney didn't disappoint. The castle lighting was amazing. We took as many pictures as we could, then headed home to upload the video. It was a "work trip" so there was no time to stay around for personal enjoyment, but I was already looking forward to going back again.

While we were there, I got to see a rougher side of Disney. People were crowded in front of the castle, trying to get a great spot for the show, and a fist fight broke out. Right at the castle, right in front of all those families and children. The cast members sprang into action and got things under control pretty fast, but it was still shocking to see. So many new experiences have come out of this move so far, I was always cautiously wondering what was next.

Another Christmas first for us was getting to finally see the Osborne Family Spectacle of Dancing Lights, over at Hollywood Studios, which was also kicking off that same week. From everything I had heard and read, we knew that we wanted to be there in the Streets of America when they first flipped the switch and the lights began. We were standing right in the middle of the street waiting with anticipation, and when Santa Goofy came out to hit the switch … all I can say is "wow." You literally are encompassed with Christmas magic, it's like nothing I had ever seen before. Classic Christmas music plays while the lights "dance" right along. Never before had I realized what I was actually missing by not going to Disney World at Christmas time. I only wish we would have gone sooner, as the lights weren't going to be around much longer. Again, the only part that felt strange to me was standing in a Christmas wonderland in warm temperatures. That really does take some getting used to.

Christmas at Disney lived up to expectations. I only wished my family from home could have been there to see it with me. In the midst of all of this fun, a friend of mine who does a YouTube show asked me to be his guest of the month for December. I agreed, but had no idea what it was that I agreed to. When we went to shoot the show, he asked me if I've ever acted before. I think I just crinkled my nose at him and said, "Umm, no." I was afraid to ask why. He had the idea of doing a skit at the opening of the show, with me playing the Fairy Godmother who was upset that Elsa from *Frozen* was going to light the Castle. And not only be upset … but we were going to blow the castle up. He couldn't be serious, right? He was. (In retrospect, given today's political climate, not the brightest idea.) I took queues from him, swallowed my pride, and took yet another flying leap out of my beloved comfort zone. And you know what? It came out pretty good. The interview part was great, he asked me about TMSM, the move, our fans, all of it. It was something that I know my parents would be proud of.

At Thanksgiving time it started to feel a bit more like home, in that the weather had gotten pretty cold, but Florida cold, not Michigan cold. The newscasters made such a big deal about the temps, which were set to fall into the upper 30s overnight. To us northerners, that's nothing. To Floridians, it's widespread panic and a mad rush to buy space heaters and blankets. It was kind of funny to see. We were pros at dealing with the cold, but others down here weren't taking it so well. Restaurants had big heaters outside. Servers wore gloves and scarves, and that was when the temps were around 60 degrees. It's surely a whole new world down here.

The week of Thanksgiving we were invited to another media event for Off TMSM, Christmas at the Gaylord Palms Resort. I had no idea what that was all about, but was very happy to be asked to go. The event featured a Christmas show and an ice display walkthough with temps kept at 9 degrees to ensure the ice sculptures stayed in finished form. They do give you jackets to wear, but the temperature in there wasn't too bad for us; we were used to the cold. After the walkthrough, they had ice tubing and tables filled with desserts and hot cocoa. This media stuff was pretty fun, not only for us being able to attend, but to gather more information for our readers.

Thanksgiving Day was a little bittersweet. While we were very thankful for making it past five months in Florida, it stung a little bit having to have Thanksgiving dinner alone. Normally we'd be with all of our extended family, and that year, there were only four of us at the dinner table. As usual, we made the best of it, had a traditional turkey dinner, and tried to have a good time. I knew the next holiday was one we'd be home for, and that was a great consolation.

After Thanksgiving we were invited to Legoland Florida. We had other events lined up for Off TMSM, so we just needed to keep everything straight and get all of our ducks in a row, before we left for Christmas back home. It's funny because we moved to Florida to be closer to Disney World and report on everything that they have to offer, but we were actually getting invited to other attractions in the area. It was mostly a good thing. Mostly.

Another invite came from Sea World, but this time it was to check out their Christmas festivities, yet another event that we had never been to. That day I encountered more bullying online, which made me not want to go that evening. Once again, I sat there and struggled with myself on what to do. Do I stand up to others in my field, hold my head up high and go where I'm invited anyway? Or do I just save myself the heartache and stay home? A friend called me that afternoon and told me if I stay home, then they win. She was right. We rounded up the boys and went to Sea World, just as planned. It was hard. Normally in "real" life if I know someone has issues with me, I would do everything I could to fix it. In the Disney business, though, you can't do that. People don't need a reason to dislike you, and it's a hard pill to swallow. This wasn't just about hiding from people who hurt me, it was about pushing forward for the greater good of my business, I had to find a way to rise above it. One of my sponsors was there that night, and we ended up enjoying the evening. Sea World is truly beautiful for Christmas. My only regret was that my children had to see people giving us the cold shoulder and the dirty looks. They didn't understand. I didn't understand it, either. Why do that? How do you explain to your kids that bullying doesn't stop as you get older, and that it doesn't always get better? I'm a fixer, a people pleaser, but there was nothing I could do about any of it. I was so ready to go home, but knew I couldn't for a bit longer. I was questioning if this job was something I was cut out for, because at the time, I sure wasn't feeling like I could handle the pressure. I'm only telling you this because I want people to understand that every job has a darker side, even when it deals with Disney and "magic."

I knew I had more to do, then we'd get to go home. I needed that. Work pressed on, and once again I needed to attend an event for a work trip. This time it was the ABC Christmas Parade taping at the Magic Kingdom. I've watched the parade on Christmas Day many times, but I never actually was there to see all that went into the production. It was a lot of standing around, but we got to see some concert taping, and were standing on the parade route, which actually landed us on television on Christmas morning, so that was a thrill. Seeing how a major network production comes together is fascinating, and gave us a new appreciation on how well Disney puts things together.

CHAPTER EIGHTEEN

Wrapping Things Up and Going Home

The week before Christmas vacation, we attended our very first Mickey's Very Merry Christmas Party at the Magic Kingdom. This was new to us, just like the Halloween party, so we were looking forward to it. The Christmas party is a fun time. The kids enjoyed the parade, especially the toy soldiers, the holiday fireworks were outstanding, and we got to meet some characters that we'd never met before, like Sandy Claws, Captain Jack Sparrow, and the Country Bears. The meet and greets were fun, but one part of the evening was particularly a good time for the kids, which surprised me. The Country Bear dance party. We stood back and watched some great character interaction, and those bears actually got my boys to dance with them. That has to be some kind of Disney magic, because it's never happened before.

Later that week we were invited to a Christmas party at Epcot, but the temps were chilly and we all had colds from being out at the Magic Kingdom late a few nights prior. I was burnt out. All the emotions of being away from home, and dealing with the struggles of the move, plus the competitiveness of the Disney business here in Florida … well, I was just done. Over it. I wanted to go home. But first, we had one more visit to attend to.

Corey and his family were in town, and even though we were leaving for Michigan in a few days, we went and did the monorail loop with them, visiting the three resorts outside the Magic Kingdom, to see the beautiful Christmas decorations. I didn't feel stressed that night. Corey and his wife are great to be around, and I knew soon we'd be heading for home. All was right in my world at that point. While at the Grand Floridian, we saw our friend Chuck, the PhotoPass cast member, who was taking pictures near the big Christmas tree. He was busy doing the job that he loved, but we snuck up and surprised him. He was happy to see us. After he took a group photo of our crew, he pulled me aside. Chuck said that I looked tired, and he was right. But it was more than that, he knew I was a bit run down, he could read me sometimes, just like my dad. They actually were the same age, and reminded me of one another. Before leaving, he gave me a hug, wished us a safe trip and a Merry Christmas, and reminded me that we did indeed have family here waiting for us when we returned. He said exactly the right thing.

The night before we left, we drove across town to drop our cat off at Mike and Janel's house, as they were going to babysit for us while we were gone for the holidays. It must have been a popular sentiment, but Janel said the same thing to me that Chuck did, that I looked tired. She told me that maybe going home to regroup and recharge is what I needed, and I think that was the case.

In the morning, we began our 18-hour ride back to Michigan. The truck was packed, with our bulldog Jack in tow, and we were on our way. The drive is long, but we were ready to take it on. Christmas is all about family, and I couldn't bear the thought of not being with them all, so we didn't mind. As we drove farther north, it felt a bit colder out at each stop. I remember we were driving in Kentucky, and I put my hand on the window and it was ice cold. Also, we could smell the aroma of wood fireplaces burning off in the distance, and home felt closer than ever. It was great. We stopped in Kentucky overnight, as we were exhausted, plus we had work to do. What some don't realize is that when we are going to be off the grid for a bit, we have to schedule posts, blogs, and all social media, just as if we were right there working on it. Some have asked me in the past if I ever sleep, when in reality I just schedule posts around the clock. We even re-post blogs overnight so our UK readers never miss anything due to the time difference.

After resting up in Kentucky, we had a roughly five-hour drive to get to my parents' house. In addition to looking forward to seeing family, we were also looking forward to some of the comfort foods from home. When we were somewhere in mid-Ohio, we saw a sign for Tim Horton's. Now, this was a big deal, as we love that place, and they unfortunately don't have one in Florida. Needless to say, an extra stop was made for some donuts and and iced cappuccino. I was already feeling better. We arrived in my parents' driveway sometime in the middle of the afternoon, tired but happy to be home. It was cold, but it finally felt like Christmas. After a lot of visiting, and even more eating, we had some Christmas shopping to do.

Christmas Eve was at my aunt's house that year, and after going to church with my parents, that's where we headed. It had been a whopping six months since I had seen my extended family, and I seriously couldn't wait to see everyone. When we arrived at my aunt's house, we hurried inside. It's weird, when you are away from family and you do finally see them, the hugs are a bit longer, the appreciation for them seems to increase. My grandma was in the kitchen fussing with the finger foods on the counter. I hugged her tighter than I ever had before, and I cried.

On Christmas day we got up, the kids opened presents, and my dad cooked his traditional Christmas dinner. Scott and I didn't really give anyone a definite day that we were leaving to go back to Florida; we sort of were playing things by ear. Plus, I think he didn't want to push the issue, as I was so glad to be home on a break from all that we left back in Florida. After Christmas was over, we shopped some sales, ate at some of our favorite restaurants (including pizza and Chinese food), and went out for dinner with friends, then over to a martini bar. I hadn't had a night out like that in months; it was a lot of fun.

Time was running out, however, and New Year's Eve was approaching, and I knew we'd have no choice but to get ready to head south again soon. Being at my parents house for the holidays made me feel like a kid again. It was comforting and safe. My mom and dad had a party at their house on New Year's Eve. We ate some good food, had some cocktails, and rang in the New Year together. I had another one of those moments, like I used to have at Disney World, when I wanted to remember certain moments before leaving our vacation. It was all reversed now. Instead of remembering magical vacation moments, I was trying to burn those important family times in my head, so I'd always know how precious they are.

The night before we were to head back to Florida, we stayed home with my parents, ordered another pizza, and had a few last-minute visitors. My parents looked a little sad before bed, and I felt the same way. Our visit was great, but it went by fast. My mother was still having issues with headaches, so I was worried about leaving her as well. When Scott and I went up to bed, I was laying awake, in my old bedroom, and the panic set in. We had been through so much since moving to Florida; it was much harder than I thought it would be, and the thought of going back scared me to death. Something was wrong, if I was having a full-blown panic attack because I had to go back.

When we got up in the morning and packed the car, it was time to say goodbye. My father is the king of pep talks, and he gave me a lot to think about on the long car ride back to Florida. He reminded me that I'm stronger than I think, and that I'm not a quitter. Sometimes when we face adversity, quitting seems much easier, but in the long run, it's not the right thing to do. People can only make you feel as bad as you allow them to, and I needed to buck up. He was right. Then we were off.

The truck needed gas, so we stopped at a gas station attached to a Tim Horton's, right off of the I-75 on ramp. We got some donuts and coffee for the road, and off we went. The weather was freezing cold that morning, and about forty minutes into Ohio, we blew a tire. Was it a sign? Were we not supposed to be leaving yet? It took us hours to get out of Ohio, between finding someone to help us, getting the truck to a repair shop, and waiting for the work to be done. Needless to say, we didn't get very far that day, and ended up stopping in Tennessee for the evening. Scott was close to just driving back to my parent's house and trying to leave again in a day or two. But having to say goodbye once was bad enough.

The next morning we knew it was going to be a long travel day, roughly ten hours. This gave me a lot of time to think. So many thoughts ran through my head while I was driving. Was I going to let insecurity and fear get the best of me, or was I going to arrive back in Florida refreshed and ready to kick some butt? It only took me till the Florida/Georgia line to come to the conclusion that fear wasn't going to win. I'm not sure what happened, but I got a sense of renewed self confidence, and I was ready to get back to doing well, regardless of what anyone said. Going away was what I needed, but vacation time was over, and it was time to return to the swing of things.

As we got closer to the house, off in the distance I could see Cinderella Castle, still lit up for Christmas, and it was a welcome sight. It gave me a feeling of being home, too. Was it possible to feel at home in two different places, so vastly different and far apart? Maybe so. I was still figuring it all out.

We made it back to Florida safe and sound. After a good night's sleep, the next day we got up and did our Florida Christmas, meaning the presents we left behind for the kids were waiting under the tree, so they had another Christmas day. Scott and I opened our presents to each other as well, even though it was early January. The weather was in the upper 70s, so we put our winter coats away and returned to Florida living.

CHAPTER NINETEEN

Let's Do This

Almost immediately upon returning to Florida, duty called. When the kids went back to school, we had to run over to Hollywood Studios to get photos of the sorcerer's hat, as word had spread that it was being taken down. With my renewed faith in our business and what we wanted to accomplish, I was getting back into work mode pretty quickly. Among all that happened in December, one thing Scott kept mentioning was his desire to to take TMSM to the next level by launching a digital magazine. Actually, he had talked about it since before we moved, but I kept brushing it off. I wasn't sure if it was doable. When he brought it up again over the holidays, I think I was still on overload, and didn't want to even think about launching another project. So, at this point, I was willing to hear him out a little bit more, and thought we could put it on the to-do list for that year, if possible.

I let the bad consume me so much at times, that the good things get lost in the background. Yes, the first six months in Florida had a lot of challenges, many ups and downs, but once I stopped to think about it, I realized that the good times were so much bigger than the bad. Even though we started The Main Street Mouse years ago, it was much more real now. We actually got to meet the people who help us and support us, and they were counting on us. I didn't want to let anyone down, so I told Scott I was going to make a conscious effort to change my way of thinking and try to focus on the positive aspects of this job.

About a week or so after getting back into town, we were invited to go to the Magic Kingdom to meet up with some Main Streeters to see the Christmas lights one more time before they were taken down for the year. They still had Christmas decorations up at Disney, and the air was cool, but it didn't feel like January. My dad texted me a picture of their driveway, and his car was covered with snow. I think the text said "trade ya!" I missed my family already, but I didn't miss dealing with scraping car windows or shoveling snow. We got our last bit of winter fix that night at the park. We met up with the group, went on some rides, had dinner together at Cosmic Ray's, and had a great time. I was happy to be there.

In the spirit of trying new things and exploring outside the Disney bubble, we finally bought annual passes for Universal Studios Orlando. We had been to CityWalk many times, but hadn't gone inside the parks, it was more like window shopping. Disney fans jokingly call Universal Studios the "dark side," but I was excited to be able to check things out; it had been years since I had been there last. They were running a special for Florida residents, so we couldn't pass up the deal. As much as our family loves Disney, the kids were itching to ride some actual roller coasters, and Universal has them, in addition to other great attractions. I was especially curious about Diagon Alley and the Wizarding World of Harry Potter. I wasn't a Harry Potter fan, and had never watched a Potter film from start to finish, but Universal did well with the theming. You don't have to be a huge fan to appreciate all that they've done. We went on the Escape from Gringotts ride, and it was amazing—so amazing that we were discussing how Disney needed to step up their game when it comes to park rides and attractions.

We needed passes not just for fun, but to be able to keep expanding content for Off TMSM. Speaking of that, we were invited to a press conference at a local theme park for the announcement of Gator Spot, an extension of Gatorland. The news media was there, the mayor of Orlando, and the president and CEO of Gatorland who spoke a bit about the company's history. It was exciting to be in the mix with the press. Once the presentation was over, I got the nerve up to talk to Mark, the CEO of Gatorland, and he was humble and gracious. Sometimes it's a little scary to push yourself, to be a bit more forward, but I was glad I talked to him. Disney is the main focus of The Main Street Mouse, but many of the businesses in the Orlando area were reaching out to us. The year was off to a decent start.

Another opportunity came up that we jumped at, and it was again for Off TMSM. One thing that's always been on my bucket list was to swim with dolphins. Dolphins are so sweet, and we love them in our household; Aidan even has stuffed dolphins in his room. We had been invited to Sea World and saw the dolphins swimming and playing in their designated area, but I never thought I'd get the chance for a personal encounter. Lucky for us, that was about to change.

The nice folks at Discovery Cove (an extension of Sea World Orlando) sent us an invitation to come out and spend the day there to come explore their park, and yes, swim with their dolphins. It was an experience unlike any other. The weather was a pinch chilly, but the staff gets you into a wetsuit, shows you a quick introduction video, and off you go with your assigned group. When we finally got in the water, I could feel a lump in my throat. The trainer called a dolphin over and there it was, right in front of us, letting us pet him. The groups are small, and we got to interact with two dolphins. Scott went first when it came time for the "swim." They tell you to swim out a bit, then a dolphin comes up, you gently hold his fin, and he brings you back to shore. What an experience. Dolphins are smart, and the trainers at Discovery Cove do a great job with them. I could never branch out like this in Michigan. Extra perspective really helps.

Staying focused is sometimes hard when you live in such a busy place. In and around Orlando, it's hard to ever feel bored. There's always something to do. We had been here for roughly 8 months, and it was starting to feel more like home, rather than an extended vacation. The boys loved their school, were making new friends, and enjoying what the area has to offer. The biggest downside was the cost of living but we were trying our best to get by. Mind over matter, head high, keep it positive, don't focus on the negative. At least that's what I was telling myself.

The seasons really don't change much in Florida. It goes from super hot to not-so-hot, that's about it. But we always have sunshine, and let's not forget the palm trees ... and Mickey Mouse. I was happy to be where I was, and had a new determination to make things work. We kept busy because of all the construction that was going on at Disney. The sorcerer's hat was over half down at Hollywood Studios, the hub at Magic Kingdom was all construction walls and there was even a box around the *Partners* statue, and Animal Kingdom was even worse. Disney had a ton of projects going on, and I was grateful that we lived close enough to keep checking on their progress. Work trips were more frequent, but busy is good. People were enjoying the up-to-date coverage on all the changes and progress over at Disney, and I was happy to be able to share all my findings with them.

CHAPTER TWENTY

Another First

Another first was coming up, and I was dreading it. My birthday was on the horizon, and I had never been away from home for that. Since I was a little girl, my mom would make me a cake, usually with hearts on it since my birthday is the day before Valentine's Day. As I got older, she'd have us over for cake and ice cream, or we'd at least go out for a big family dinner. We never missed a birthday together … until now.

One thing that I'd never done was to celebrate my birthday at Disney World, and I've always wanted to. Scott knew darn well that I was going to have a rough day, so he planned out an entire day to keep me busy. There was also another surprise in the works. Little did I know, when I woke up on the morning of my birthday, I had a special blog waiting for me. Autumn, my friend and head admin on the site, asked my family back home, fellow staffers, and other friends to write me a birthday message. She compiled all of these messages together so I'd have it first thing that day. How nice is that? I got up and sat on the couch, then Scott put my computer on my lap and opened up the blog. I sat there and bawled my eyes out, reading message after message. It was one of the nicest things that anyone had done for me, and I was thankful. Scott also wrote a special blog for me, which meant so much.

After composing myself, the phone rang and it was my parents. Every year on my birthday, my mom's first words to me have always been, "Happy Birthday, Birthday Girl!" and lo and behold, when I answered the phone, that's exactly what I heard. She never disappoints. More tears fell, but my parents again reminded me of how proud they were of me, and to enjoy my birthday and not be sad. Plus, it was about 2 degrees in Michigan, so that bit of info helped a little, too. My first Florida birthday was off to a great start, and my heart was full and thankful. Things were just getting started....

Since I had never had a real Disney birthday, Scott wanted to do as much as we could to get the full experience. The first stop of the day was the Grand Floridian Resort for breakfast with some fun Disney characters at their buffet, 1900 Park Fare. In all the months we've lived in Florida, we still hadn't done a character breakfast, so I was excited. The food at 1900 Park Fare was awesome, lots of delicious choices, and not the place to go if you're trying to stick to a diet, which I blew that day for sure. Mickey waffles, cheesy eggs, omelettes, pastries, fresh fruit, yogurt.... The characters were fantastic, too. We took pictures with Pooh, Tigger, Alice, the Mad Hatter, and Mary Poppins, who told my boys that they had proper manners. When we were finished, our server brought me a Mickey cupcake and they all sang Happy Birthday to me. I seriously couldn't have asked for a better morning.

After the breakfast fun, we hopped on the monorail and headed to the Magic Kingdom to keep the celebration going. We arrived at my favorite park, and I finally got to do something I always wanted to do: wear a birthday button at Disney. It may sound small, but it was exciting to me. After hearing a few birthday wishes from various cast members, I saw that there was no line for Princess Aurora, who was up front that day. I normally don't stand in line for girlie characters since I always have the boys in tow, but it was my day, and they didn't mind. The family and I walked around, went on some of my favorite rides, got a Starbucks treat (where they also make a big deal over birthdays, I found out), watched the Festival of Fantasy Parade, and overall had a magical day. Disney really does it right when it comes to making guests feel special on their birthday. I've gone to Disney more times than I can count, but I have never felt as joyful and happy as I did that day. It was true Disney magic.

We ended our day at Chef Mickey's at the Contemporary. Yes, two character buffets in one day. By the time we got home, we were all exhausted; it had been quite an adventure. Firsts are hard, and I was dreading my first birthday away from home, but the day turned out to be beyond fantastic. My husband and kids did a great job of keeping my mind occupied so that I'd have a memorable day ... and I sure did.

The following day was Valentine's Day. Scott wanted to keep the weekend going, so we went to CityWalk for dinner and ate at

Margaritaville. Another favorite. They even gave me a birthday button at Universal, but it's not the same as at Disney. You can see the difference on how they do things for guests.

As if I wasn't tired enough from all the activities of Friday and Saturday, I was told on Sunday morning that I needed to get myself together, because we had to meet a business associate over at the Magic Kingdom. I was dragging behind a bit, and really wanted to take the day to rest, but work takes priority so I went with the flow.

Once we got inside the park, I realized that we were not meeting a business associate. Instead, there was a little surprise party waiting for me at the train station in the front of the park. My Florida friends were all there. It speaks volumes on who truly cares about you when you see acts of kindness like this. They were so worried about me feeling lonely being away from home, that they made it a point to make sure I knew they were there for me. After I gave everyone hugs, I was told that they got to the park a few hours prior to stake out a prime spot for the parade, which is one of my favorites. It was nice to have everyone together.

After the parade, we went down to the front of the park to find me another birthday button to wear for the day. The cast member who gave me my button was coincidentally a member of TMSM, so that was humbling to hear. Speaking of cast members, a large group of them came up to us as we ate lunch at Cosmic Ray's and sang "Happy Birthday" to me. Even more magic, and yes, someone in our group recorded it so I'd have that memory as a keepsake. We went on some rides together, stopped to see my friend Lorraine who was working in Tomorrowland, and had an awesome day together.

Sometimes when you feel a little scared or alone, you get a beautiful reminder that you are indeed *not* alone, and there's nothing to be scared of. That's what these people did for me that day. The move to Florida and settling in here has been an incredible journey, filled with ups and downs, and wasn't always easy. People aren't always nice. But that day, at different times, I'd say each of them told me at some point that I'm not alone, that my family and I are loved, and that was the best gift they could have given me.

Firsts are always hard, and there had been a lot of them in less than a year's time. All you can do is take it in stride and hope for the best. That was the plan for us.

CHAPTER TWENTY-ONE

Family First

After a magical birthday weekend, it was time to get back to work. Spring was in the air at Disney World, even though most of the rest of the country was freezing. Epcot was getting ready to kick off their yearly Flower and Garden Festival, so we had to get pictures and info for the site. Since we used to be Disney creatures of habit when we vacationed, I never had seen the Flower and Garden Festival in person. Our travel time was always around Labor Day, year after year, so we didn't realize how many things we were actually missing. Seeing these types of festivities online or in photos truly don't do them justice. The character topiaries at Epcot are gorgeous. The area near the monorail track was filled with flowers, which gave off a lovely scent of spring. The Florida weather had really been all over the place, but I couldn't complain after hearing how cold my family and friends were back at home.

Even though my new "gratitude attitude" was helping, and the year was going great, I was missing home. Talking to my parents on the phone was helpful, but I really wished I could see them more than just every few months. I made the mistake of looking at pictures from the year prior on Facebook, and got a bit emotional. When I was still in Michigan the previous winter I was freezing, wishing that I could be in Florida. So sometimes you can't win, there are good and bad points to everything.

TMSM was doing well and growing daily, which made me feel even better about this big adventure we were on. Business meetings were coming up, we were making some great contacts, everything was as good as I hoped for, but things were about to change.

My mother had been having some health issues on and off since we moved, but she was being proactive about it and going to the doctor, so I tried not to worry. The doctors kept saying she had shingles, but she wasn't getting better, only worse. Her headaches were to the point that she could barely more, so my dad decided that they needed to see a specialist and took her to a neurologist. On a Friday afternoon I got a frantic phone call, one that I wasn't ready for. My mother was having surgery on her brain at the beginning of the next week. They found the cause of her pain, and were going to move on it right away. This was one of the biggest fears I had about moving: that something would be wrong with my parents, or another close family member, and I wouldn't be there for them. That fear was staring me in the face and I was heartbroken. After getting details from my dad, I spoke to my mom, who was scared about her upcoming surgery. She told me that she had to have it done at a hospital that she wasn't familiar with, in downtown Detroit, and the procedure was going to take the entire day. My mom has always been pretty selfless, and instead of worrying about her own well being, she was concerned about my father having to sit at the hospital alone that day. She didn't want him to do that, just in case something bad happened. To hear her cry broke me in half. So what did I do? I packed my bags and went home. I didn't even think twice about it. Disney will always be there, I have a great staff that will man the ship for me in my absence, and my priority became making sure my parents were taken care of.

The next day when I got back to Michigan, my poor mom was in such pain, I was afraid to hug her. You couldn't even go anywhere near her head. She looked so tired, but so did my dad. They had been through so much. My mom had been sicker than they wanted me to know, and I really had no idea what I was walking into. Her concern again was my dad. She started telling me what she needed me to do, in case something happened to her. I didn't want to hear any of that; the possibility of losing one of them was too much to bear, so I tried to keep her talking about positive things, and how the surgery was sure to be a success.

On the day of her surgery, we had to be downtown by 6 am. It was early, but I don't think any of us slept well durning the night. My dad and I sat in the waiting room while they prepped my mom for surgery, then let us see her. Keeping a tough exterior for your family goes along with that whole reversal thing I was talking about before. Usually it's them who have had to be strong for me, and now the shoe was on the other foot. We told her we loved her, that it was going to be okay, and that we'd see her later in the evening. There was nothing more we could do other than pray that God gave the surgeon the guidance to fix her and get her back to normal.

It was going to be a long day, but I was in it for the duration with my dad. We chatted about so many things, and he kept saying he was glad I was there. There was no place else I would rather be. We went to find food, browsed the gift shop, paced the waiting room floor ... the day was dragging. No updates were coming about my mom, and she had been back there for hours. Finally, a nurse called us into a room to wait. Even though we only sat there waiting for maybe ten minutes, it felt like forever. The doctor was done with her her procedure, and was coming to tell us how it went. I just kept praying...

When the doctor finally came in, he had a straight face, and my heart sank. Little did I know that he always looks like that. My worry was quickly gone, as he told us that her surgery was a success. The doctor said it would be awhile before she wakes up, and told us to go grab a snack and they'd let us know when we could see her. So, dad and I went to the cafeteria for a bit. As we were sitting there, the doctor came down to talk to us again, to reassure us that in time, she's going to be back to her old self. It was nice of him to do that; we needed those kind words.

Eventually, they called us in to go see her, and it was a bag of mixed emotions. We knew she was going to recover, but it was hard to see her, with her head bandaged up, hooked up to machines. It was awful. When she woke up, she was groggy and in pain. My brother Greg and soon-to-be sister-in-law Amee came up to see her, too, but she mostly slept. She had to stay in the hospital for most of the week, but we spent almost the whole time there with her. Once she got home, we tried to set up shop for her in her bedroom, and make her comfortable. I couldn't stay much longer, as I had to get back to Florida. By the time I left, she was making some progress, my dad was getting some relief, and things were beginning to look up.

Thank God I was able to go home when they needed me. The site did fine, Scott and our staff had my back, and I was hopeful for my parents to get back to somewhat of a normal life soon. They did have plans to visit Florida in April, but I knew that was going to depend on my mom's recovery. Time would tell.

CHAPTER TWENTY-TWO

Spring Has Sprung

Shortly after I returned to Florida, summer weather was back, and we started to have some really hot days. One afternoon I was mowing the lawn thinking, 'It's March, it's way too early for this.' In Michigan, we normally don't worry about yard work until at least May. I wasn't complaining, though—after the stressful time in Michigan, a little sunshine is just what was needed. With warmer weather here and spring break looming, the Orlando area was getting busier and busier. The parks were slammed with people, lines were long, and it felt like summer had arrived a few months too soon. Speaking of spring break, the school schedules here are different from Michigan, just like they were at the beginning of the school year. In Michigan, spring break coincides with Easter. It's usually the week after Easter, and we get Good Friday off. Down here in Florida, the break is in March, with no time off at Easter. That was an adjustment.

When the kids had the week off, we tried to keep them busy. The crowd levels were high, but we made the best of it. One of our sponsors at the time gave me some photography lessons, so we were taking the camera out and about more to get pics for the site, especially at Epcot for the Flower and Garden Festival. My older son Andrew took a liking to the butterfly tent that they had; he had butterflies landing on his hand. While in there, he started asking me how to take pictures of them and have it come out clear. I was still learning the ins and outs of picture taking, but I started to teach him what I knew. Kids can get into bad habits or spend hours on video games, so his interest in photography was good news. I was happy to share the learning with him. This would prove useful later on.

The Easter season was quickly upon us, and we got to see the extras that Disney World does to celebrate. One of the best things they offer is the chocolate egg display at the Grand Floridian. I had never seen them before, so we were sure to head over and get photos once the display was up. These huge chocolate eggs were carved with scenes from beloved Disney movies, with favorite characters on them. And the smell ... the lobby has a faint aroma of chocolate to it. Doesn't get much better than that. Also in April, my friend Autumn was in town again, and we had some activities planned with her and her husband. We went to visit the Easter Bunny at the Magic Kingdom, and were able to try out the new breakfast offerings at the Be Our Guest restaurant. We don't usually do much dining at Disney, mostly counter service. If we're having company in town or there's a special occasion, we try to make arrangements to eat a little better. The breakfast at Be Our Guest was new, so even though we were going with friends, it was also a work trip. I wanted to get photos for our readers, as they were asking for details.

Another bit of work we did was staking out the Polynesian Resort, as there were ramblings of the new patio, Grog's Grotto, and associated bar, Trader Sams, doing a soft opening that weekend. We got some photos and a bit of information, plus it was nice having someone to help cover Disney happenings.

After Autumn went home, Easter was next. Usually on Easter, we would go to church, then have dinner with family. Not this year, of course. I felt a pinch sad, but not as much as I thought I would, because I got the news that my parents were coming to town for their scheduled visit. They weren't sure because my mom was still recovering from surgery, but she said she wanted to visit, and that the warmth and sunshine would do her good. That was great news.

Even though our schools were done with spring break here, the rest of the country was only just beginning theirs. I remember when I was younger, Florida was always my destination of choice when it came to vacations. It's different to view it from the other side, from a local's perspective. Traffic was heavier, theme parks were even more crowded than usual, even restaurants around Disney property had lines out the door. I saw a lot of Michigan license plates on the road, and I smiled, because I used to be just like them. Vacation time? Florida it is!

Speaking of vacations, my parents made their way back to town the following weekend, too. Before getting ready for company, we had work to do first. TMSM was given media passes for MegaCon, the big comic book convention here in Orlando. Motor City Comic

Con was the only one I was familiar with, but Orlando's is bigger, and I was excited to check things out. Even after being a Disney fan my entire life, I was still pretty new to the convention scene. Scott, on the other hand, was a regular, even before he met me, so he had to show me the ropes. When we got to the convention, it was insanity. People were dressed up as their favorite characters, they had retail booths everywhere inside the convention center, food, and of course my favorite, the row of celebrity tables. The comic community is enormous, and these events are a big deal for fans. They had a whole section of Star Wars props from the various movies, along with memorabilia, which got me a bit more excited to be experiencing our first Star Wars Weekends that were coming up at Hollywood Studios. Back on celebrity row, each media guests is different, as to whether they'll let members of the press approach them or take pictures. Some did, some didn't.

I'm a huge fan of AMC's *The Walking Dead*, and they had some cast members there. Norman Reedus, who plays Darryl Dixon, had a huge crowd in his area. I could see the top of his hat, and that was about it. All I wanted was a closer picture, so I asked his handler if it would be okay. She told me to wait, and a few minutes later she came back and told me to follow her. We walked right up to the front of the table, and they let me take photos of him. I didn't want to upset the people in line, so I took pictures as quick as I could, then got out of the way. Another celebrity who allowed photos, and who we met, was Lou Ferrigno, the first actor to portray the Incredible Hulk. He was very nice.

Work trips like that are tiring, but they're fun. We head out to gather as much info as we can, take pictures, then go home and write it all up. It's a long process, but it's one that I'm always happy to do. We are always thankful when we get media invitations, and try to do as many of them as we can.

My family got here on Saturday afternoon. After my mom being so sick, it was great seeing her up and about. She wasn't feeling one hundred percent yet, so we took things slow. On Sunday we took them to Epcot for a few hours, and took them on Soarin' for the first time. They loved it, my dad especially. We didn't stay long, as my mom was tiring pretty fast. Animal Kingdom was another park we hit that they had never been to while they were in town. Again, we only stayed a few hours, but they got to see the Festival of the

Lion King, and I talked my dad into going on Expedition Everest. The last part of their stay, we went over to Port Orleans Riverside, and took the boat over to Downtown Disney, which was just about to become Disney Springs. This was a nice, relaxing activity for them, and something they enjoyed.

The visit went by fast, but I was thankful to see my mom doing a lot better, and she and my dad were getting back to somewhat normal. The next time I was to see them would be summer, so it was pretty safe to say that by then, she'd be good as new. At least that was our hope.

CHAPTER TWENTY-THREE

On the Scene

After our company left, we had to get back to work, as Disney had a lot coming up on their schedule. But first, we had a busy few days coming up, with media events for Off TMSM.

When we first got to town, we made a great media contact with a man named John, who was the marketing manager at the new I-Drive 360 Complex that was being built. At this location, a whole new entertainment area was coming which included the Sea Life Aquarium, Madame Tussaud's Wax Museum, and the Orlando Eye, a roughly 400-foot observation wheel. The first time we were invited out by John, the wheel was only just beginning to be built. He gave Scott and I hard hats and we toured the construction area. Only the base of the wheel was up at that time. We were hoping that we'd be asked back once the complex was completed, and in fact we were. John was one of the first people in the area to give us a shot when we arrived in Florida, and he was always good to us, so I wanted to cover these events well.

It was a whirlwind three days. The first media day was for the Sea Life Aquarium. They gave people from the media different times to attend the walkthrough, so it wasn't too crowded, and allowed people enough space to take photos. The following day, and one I was looking forward to, was Madame Toussaud's Orlando. We arrived at the complex and waited with other press outside for them to let us inside. This was probably the first time in months that I had to face my fears and deal with others in the community who weren't so nice to us. If you recall, the old me in December had a knotted-up stomach, and was ready to stay home and hide. Fast forward a few months, the new and improved me was standing there, holding my head high, and didn't give a rip about the whispers and dirty looks. How's that for progress? Another lesson learned, that you may also find useful, is that confidence causes an exchange of power. If you allow people to run you off, they will. I wasn't going to let that happen, and still have that philosophy today.

As we walked through the wax museum, we turned a corner and came face to face with ... Walt Disney! Or rather, his wax figure. It was sad to think that Walt's vision and ideas grew to the size that they did, and he wasn't here to see it. As we continued through, we saw more of our favorite celebrities represented.

Our three days of media madness was to close out the next day, with the opening of the Orlando Eye. Before they allowed the press to actually ride it, there was a "walk the wheel" stunt about to happen, and daredevil Nic Wallenda was going to balance his way across one of the beams, with no safety net. My friend Janel went with me to cover this one, as we had to be there early and Scott took the kids to school and was going to meet up with us later. As we stood there watching him walking, hundreds of feet off the ground, awful thoughts were running though my head, and I was scared for him. I was trying to do a live feed for our viewers, and hold my hand as still as I could, even though I was a jittery mess watching that.

Afterward, we went inside, and the aquarium and museum was open for the press again, but with no restrictions or guides, so we went where we wanted to take more pictures and video. We went to the back of the complex once Scott got there, and we waited our turn for our capsule, as it was time to ride the Orlando Eye. I'm not a fan of heights, not at all, but this was part of the job, so I had to suck it up and deal with my phobia. The nice part is that the wheel is really smooth, and turns really slow, so it's not so bad. The view from the top is unbelievable; you can see all the theme parks in the area, and on clear days, you can see all the way to the coast.

When we got off the wheel, a local news crew was standing there. Apparently they were interviewing people as they walked off the ride. The reporter talked to us, and told me they had a lot of tapes to go through, as they had interviewed about 40 groups of people, but we could see if we made the news later that afternoon. I didn't think we had a chance. That evening we were watching the news, waiting for the section on the Orlando Eye, and to my surprise, we did make it. I'm glad Scott had the DVR set just in case. We recorded it and played it back a few times. Part of the reason for recording the footage was so that our crew back home could see it, too.

May was to be a busy month where Disney was concerned. Mother's Day weekend was filled with Disney fun, as we spent the day at the Magic Kingdom, then tried dinner at 1900 Park Fare since we enjoyed their breakfast so much. Disney passes out flowers to all the mothers who visit the resorts and parks, which is a nice touch. I was sad that I didn't get to see my mom, but my boys kept me busy and it turned out to be a nice day.

Star Wars Weekends were kicking off at Disney's Hollywood Studios, and as that we had never gone before, we were excited to check things out and cover the happenings for the site. Now, I'll admit, in the grand scheme of things, I'm not a huge *Star Wars* fan. I've seen all the movies, but I don't go overboard when it comes to the franchise. My husband and older son *are* big *Star Wars* fans, so I knew we'd be attending Star Wars Weekends more than once. I had heard so much about these weekends, and now it was time to finally get to attend for ourselves. We walked around, met characters, checked out the new merchandise, then closed out the day with the Symphony in the Stars fireworks show. Not a bad first attempt at Star Wars Weekends. Little did I know then, but it would be our first and last opening weekend, as Disney would announce later that the event was being retired.

The end of May proved to be just as busy as the beginning. Aidan was celebrating his first Florida birthday, and we wanted to him to have a good time. Disney was having their 24-hour party that weekend at the Magic Kingdom, so we decided to do a last-minute TMSM meet-up while we were there. The meet-up spot for the group photo was near the flagpole at the front of the park. While we were standing there waiting, they were getting ready for the flag retreat ceremony, and Aidan got approached by the Dapper Dans. They asked if he wanted to be their special guest and help them recite the Pledge of Allegiance. What an honor, he was thrilled, and I was on cloud nine.

After the ceremony, it was meet-up time. Even though we didn't give a huge amount of notice, we did have a decent number of people present. We socialized, walked around the park, and had fun, but we didn't make it through the night. We were home by 2:00 am, the kids were tired, but at least we can say we went. The following year Disney didn't host a 24-hour party, so as with Star Wars Weekends, it was our first and last shot as well.

CHAPTER TWENTY-FOUR

Feet on Ground, Head Elsewhere

In the midst of all this craziness, we were in serious discussions at home, too. Scott was pushing for e-magazine idea. Someone had shown him how to build it, and if we had the right content, it was something he felt we could do. I wasn't sold on the idea, because I knew it would be a lot of extra work, but eventually he wore me down and I agreed. If we wanted to expand TMSM, maybe that was the way to do it. So, behind the scenes, we were busy gathering up people to help us get content together, but I didn't want to announce it to our readers until it was almost time. Anything could happen, or we could change our minds, so I wanted to wait just to be sure. The plan was to make the magazine about all things that TMSM covers: Disney, Off TMSM, TMSM Geek (another spinoff), all of it. With the many events we were invited to in the area, I knew we could get content.

Around the same time, we were asked to attend the media press release at Sea World for the debut of Mako, a new coaster planned for the following year. While at the media day, they offered people the opportunity to see the coaster site from above, by going up in a crane 200 feet in the air. They harness you in ... and make you sign a waiver ... but it's part of the job, right? I forgot to mention, a week or so prior, I did a bungee drop at another media event, from around the same height. After reporting on the second experience, I got a message from my dad asking if I had lost my mind, and said I was making my mother nervous and to do my reporting on the ground.

June was here, and we were looking forward to school being out for the summer. We had another birthday in the house, but this time it was Andrew's turn. With all the places to visit around town, when I asked what he wanted to do for his birthday, he picked something familiar. Back in Michigan, he always chose Buffalo Wild Wings and the comic-book store for his birthday outing, and that's what he chose for his first Florida birthday, too. Maybe he was missing home a little, and wanted to do things that he was used to, but he didn't say, and I didn't push. So, that's exactly what we did, and he was happy with that. We got in a pinch more time at Star Wars Weekends, too, but it was so hot and crowded.

Once school let out, we had some of our staffers over for a BBQ. We held discussions about the magazine, and were trying to plan for its release date, which was going to be July 1 if things went well. Another project to worry about … but I didn't want to count my chickens before they hatch, so I was waiting to see how things went.

This adventure that we'd been on for almost one year had been quite a ride. More things were coming, and I was ready to go back home to see everyone. The adventure was about to hit an all-time high for me, and I didn't even realize it was coming. Let me give you a pinch of a back story....

When I was a kid, like a lot of other teens my age, I was obsessed with New Kids on the Block. I had posters all over the walls in my room, bought shirts, buttons, went to as many concerts as possible. When I was 15 I begged my dad to take my friend and I to see the band in concert for the first time, and he finally gave in and took us. Just my dad and two obnoxious girls. What a good sport he was! As I got older, I still loved them, and when they started touring again, I was sure to go. On their first reunion tour, I had emergency surgery the same week I had tickets for their concert, but I was not going to miss it. I was out of the hospital for a couple of days, but I still went. That's dedication. Or insanity. Maybe both.

Anyway, one of our business contacts who sent us press releases down here was the Amway Center, the big venue for events in downtown Orlando. Scott had contacted our media person there, once we heard that New Kids was coming to their arena. I didn't want to get my hopes up, but we had been waiting to hear if we got media passes for that evening. The night before the concert, we received an email that tickets would be waiting for us at the will-call window. To say I was excited is an understatement. The night of the concert, we picked up the tickets and there were instructions to go to the side door of the building. There were lines of people waiting, but it wasn't the main entrance. We struck up a conversation with some people in front of us, then eventually we were lead inside. The stage manager came out and told everyone to shut off their cell phones, there was a photographer on hand, and we were actually going to meet the group. With all the New Kids concerts I had attended in my life, and believe me there were plenty of them, never was there an opportunity like this. I was literally shaking; I felt like a teenager again.

Within a few minutes, all five members of New Kids appeared from behind a curtain, and the meet-and-greet part of the evening began. I was so nervous, I don't recall everything that happened, but I do know that I spoke to all of them, and that was a dream come true. When it came time for pictures, I was sure to stand near my favorite New Kid, Joey McIntyre, and thanked him for helping me cross this experience off my bucket list. I got hugs from them, then we started to walk away. Standing over to the side was Tonya, our media contact, and she had the biggest smile on her face. She arranged that for me out of the goodness of her heart, and I was so grateful.

The concert wasn't to begin for almost two hours, so when we walked outside, we ran into the girls we stood in line with, and they invited us to go hang out with them at a bar across the street to kill time. Once we got inside, the first person I called was my dad. He took me to my first New Kids concert years ago, and I wanted him to know what had happened and how happy I was. He was excited to hear that, he laughed at me because I was squealing like a kid, but he understood why.

When it was concert time, they put us up on the club level, with the other local media. It was an awesome show, and the whole experience ranks near the top of my list of things that have happened since we moved.

About two days later, I received the photo from the Amway Center that their photographer took of us and the group. There I was, standing next to Joe, with Jordan Knight on the other side of me. You can bet that I posted that online right away!

CHAPTER TWENTY-FIVE

We Made It

So, school was out, Disney was revving up for another Frozen Summer Fun run at Hollywood Studios, and we were celebrating our one-year Florida anniversary. One year. There were so many times that I didn't think we'd make it that long. So many times I'd tell myself to just get through the year, just make it that far, then re-evaluate what was happening with the site and our lives.

We had been behind the scenes working on our upcoming online magazine, and had come up with a name, *The Main Street Monthly*, but no one knew that yet. I felt like because I had been an open book with our readers every week thus far, that I wanted to write them something special that evening, something to recap our first year in Florida. It was from the heart, and was my truth at the time. Here's part of what I wrote to our Main Streeters that night:

> Believe it or not, today's blog marks ONE YEAR of Florida living for me and my family. Yes, one year ago I arrived at our new place in Florida, not knowing what was in store for us or if it was the right thing to do. Moving your family across the country is something that's not to be taken lightly, and as you know, I took it very seriously. I'm a home type of person, someone who was used to having my family and friends close by, celebrating every holiday and birthday together. How could I leave all of that behind and move so far away? Was I crazy to chase a dream? At the time, I thought maybe I was, but it's not a year later, and I've been doing a lot of reflecting on all that's happened since last June. I wasn't crazy, I was determined. I believed I could, so I did.
>
> Now, let me back up for a minute, and I wasn't always so sure of myself. Actually, I was filled with a lot of doubt. I'm not usually a risk-taker, and I rarely step out of my comfort zone. But when you have the people that you love most behind you and believing in you, it makes major decisions a little easier to make. I have learned SO much in the

past year ... about business, about others, and about myself. When I was thinking about the past year and what to write, a lot of sad memories crept into my mind. Owning your own business is hard. Actually, believe it or not, owning your own Disney-related business is ridiculously hard. This field is cutthroat and competitive, and I didn't realize how much so until I moved. I'm not used to that. Where I come from, people are a lot truer to their word when it comes to friendships, which makes it a whole lot easier to trust others. Taking people at their word and at face value was something I was used to doing, but I had to learn the hard way that in business, that's not how things work. Integrity is something that not everyone found to be as important as I did, and it was hard. Hurtful, too. All that I was used to had to change. I had to change. I had to learn to put my guard up, get stronger, and I absolutely have. That being said, instead of focusing on the hardships of the past year, let's focus on the good.

Yes, the past year has been a huge adjustment for me, I had to leave my comfortable surroundings in order to make TMSM grow and flourish ... and wouldn't you know it, The Main Street Mouse DID grow, and it HAS flourished. I was at a standstill in Michigan, I went about as far as I could go, being so far away from what my business is centered around. Sure, I had people tell me I couldn't do this, that I couldn't make TMSM more successful, that we were at a plateau. But again, I believed I could, and I did. Actually, WE did. This isn't just about me. It's about the people who helped me, who believed in and still believe in me, that's where the heart of the matter is. My husband keeps our sites running, handles all the tech issues and such, and has sacrificed for my dream. My family and friends who miss me at home knew that they had to let me go so I could see this thing through. My Disney friends, who have become like family to me, who help me every day. people who help run TMSM, who write for me, and have my back at all costs. THAT is huge. My gosh, our "fans" or readers, they are my Disney Ohana. Do you know how many amazing people I've gotten to meet since moving here, that otherwise I might not have? I finally got to meet and thank my original supporter and staff members, people who have been with us through thick and thin these past five years ... Autumn, Corey and Mike. All of us were finally together, after all this time, it was long overdue. Moving to Florida also gave us the opportunity to start Off TMSM, so we've branched out to other businesses in the area. Local business owners have been so nice and welcoming to us, which has been a huge asset in helping us grow our sites. We have a lot to be thankful for.

Since arriving in Florida, I have met hundreds of Main Streeters. It's an honor and such a humbling experience, meeting people who care about what we do here at TMSM. I don't take that lightly at all. We've done meet-ups, and each time, when I see the large turn out, it makes me cry. I still can't believe that God has blessed me with such amazing supporters, it's overwhelming. I tried to think about what makes The Main Street Mouse special, and it's not me, it's all of you. TMSM has become so much more than just a girl from Michigan with big Disney dreams, it's become a family. A really large, close-knit family. When people say they are excited to meet me, I turn it right around, because it's me who is excited to meet all of YOU. Some joke with me, because I always give people hugs when I meet them, but it's truly out of love and appreciation for you caring enough to take the time to say hello or keep up with what we do on a daily basis. I'm truly grateful.

The first year is over, and the second one is beginning. The past year has been a roller-coaster ride, but we made it through. I hope along the way that I've managed to make my family and friends proud of what we've accomplished. I can't thank you all enough for following along on our adventures, for supporting our efforts, and believing in our dreams. Speaking of dreams … learn from me. If there is something that is in your heart, that you truly want to do, believe in yourself and DO IT. I always think of Rapunzel, and the song "I've Got A Dream" from *Tangled*. We all have dreams, we all have goals. Don't ever let anyone tell you that you can't do something, because actually, you sure can. Find that inner strength, you're probably a lot tougher than you even realize. I still have my moments where I have self doubts, times when I wonder if I made the right choices, but I know it's normal to feel that way. Because of YOU, our amazing Main Streeters, along with our family and friends, you've allowed me to live my dream, and I thank you for that. You have been a blessing to me, and I'm forever grateful for your love, support and kindness. So thank you for giving me the push that I've needed this past year. I'm excited to see what the next year has in store for The Main Street Mouse, and I hope you will continue along on this journey with me.

That was only part of what I wrote that night, but I think you can get the idea of the sentiment behind it. To me, staying humble and thankful is important. Also, speaking from the heart is another important aspect of what we do at TMSM. What you see is what you get with me. I try to be fully open with our readers on how things really are and what is going on with us week after week. The more

I could do to inspire others, the more I wanted to do. The more we accomplished with the sites, the more we wanted to grow and expand. Like finally launching our magazine, for example. Our readers didn't know it yet, but it was coming, and soon. In the meantime, we kept plugging away, working as hard as we could, to cover as much as possible so our readers would have great material to check out day in and day out.

CHAPTER TWENTY-SIX

The Adventure Continues

It was getting closer to our visit back to Michigan, but we had so much to do before then. Gatorland invited us out for the day, which worked out great because we were going to do a write up on Gatorland in the first issue of *The Main Street Monthly*. I'm a girly girl, and usually don't do too many things out of the ordinary. I had promised my parents that I'd do my reporting from the ground, but at Gatorland, they had us zip lining over pits of live gators. Who can pass up that opportunity? After that, we got to feed a whole mess of gators piled up together on the shore of their pond. They have you turn your back to said gators while they take your picture with them. When my parents saw that, they thought I had finally lost my mind. Adventure is good, and so is trying new things … plus, it was a work trip, I had to do it.

Father's Day was upon us and we all went to the movies. Also on the agenda was to go see the Frozen fireworks the weekend that the summer fun event kicked off. Autumn was coming back to town, so we organized a Frozen Fun TMSM meet-up at Hollywood Studios. We had a lot going on, but I wanted to make time to do that. The last week of June, however, was all work, no play, as the July 1 release date for the magazine was almost here.

That week, we stayed in our room/office area and worked … and worked … and worked. Pretty much around the clock. Those who were helping us sent in their articles and pictures, and along with our own added content, Scott had to build the magazine and make sure it all flowed together properly. We had put off this project for so long, and now it was go time, it had to work. We wanted people to enjoy the magazine, and get behind it so that we could keep putting out issues month after month. Quality was key, and all those hours of work paid off. On July 1, *The Main Street Monthly* was released, and our readers loved it. We were exhausted, but felt such a huge sense of accomplishment.

It was "vacation" time now, as we were going home for a summer visit and a well-needed break. What was the rest of the year going to entail? I surely didn't know, but I was hopeful.

Our visit home was great, I was so happy to be home. During that visit, we had that Fourth of July party at my parents' house, the one I had missed the year before. Even though I was on vacation, I was still thinking about work, and what I wanted to do for the magazine. I started a column called "Disney in the City ~ Confessions of a Grown-up Disney Princess." The goal was to have some real girl talk, with a Disney spin. The series is still going, and does well; it's one of my favorite things to write.

We stayed long enough to celebrate my dad's birthday before heading back to Florida. I wasn't as sad leaving, because I knew we'd be back home in October for my brother's wedding. My little brother was getting married on Halloween, to a gal that I just adored. I was finally getting the sister I always wanted. We said our goodbyes, or the "see ya real soon" part, and returned to Florida. There was so much to do: the August issue of the magazine was going to be assembled, school was starting soon, and I knew that I was going to have to begin working on our second big meet-up.

Once we got back in Florida, the fast-paced life picked right back up. We needed to get back into the parks to see what we had missed. The final bits of summer were lingering, and we were starting to see Halloween merchandise creeping in here and there at the various stores across Disney World. Halloween already? Yep. We had open houses for the boys' schools, as Andrew was going to be in high school, so there was double duty now as far as school pick ups and such. Just to give them something special before school, we took them to Crystal Palace for dinner at the Magic Kingdom, which we all enjoyed. Since my brother was getting married on Halloween, I went to the Haunted Mansion store, Memento Mori, and sent my future sister-in-law some spooky kitchen goodies for the shower.

The summer was a good one. We launched the magazine, covered events, went home for a visit, spent two days at Daytona Beach ... it was all good. The kids starting school always tugs at my heart, and it did even more so that year. How could I have a child starting high school? Would he change, would he not need me so much anymore? My thoughts always get the best of me and I worry. And my little guy? Starting middle school. Time does fly, there's nothing we can do to stop it, but I don't think I was ready. I'm such a sap, I can't help it.

After buying them the usual endless amounts of supplies and uniforms, they began school and all was well. Of course my worries were for nothing ... again. One would think I'd learn. I had a moment of pause, though. If I was that upset at my boys starting milestone years at school, schools that were ten minutes away, what must it be like for my parents, seeing me move across the country? They are amazing people, and much stronger than I am. No one gives you a handbook when it comes to parenting, you just do your best. I'd like think I learned a thing or two from them. It's always a work in progress, though, like everything else.

CHAPTER TWENTY-SEVEN

Food, Wine, and Finding Time

Epcot kicked off their Food and Wine Festival. We were working hard as usual, and I had my sights set on going home for Halloween, so indulging at the Food and Wine Fest was off the table this year. Not just because it's expensive, but my bridesmaid dress came in the mail and it was way too snug. The choice was there: send it back for a bigger size and pay the alteration fee, or stop eating Disney goodies and exercise more. I chose the latter. My hope was, since the year was on an upswing, that if I could get though all the hurdles I've been through, losing some pounds would be doable, too.

People ask how we don't get fatter or go broke living so close to Disney World. The answer is simple. We can't afford it. Living near Disney and vacationing near Disney are like night and day. I never realized how much so until we moved here. One good point, if you're trying to get extra exercise and you live close to Disney, walking in the parks does wonders. Walking around a Disney Park, rather than walking around a track or neighborhood, is so much better. The scenery is nice, and you can cover a lot of miles. Also, did you know that Disney parks offer free ice water at most counter-service restaurants? I started carrying flavored powder or packets of lemon juice in my purse to jazz the water up a bit. I couldn't think of a better slim-down program!

In addition to preparing for the wedding, I also had another big meet-up to think about. Last year's festivities went so well, I wanted to put something together again, but change the location. We did Epcot for the big meet-up, and a smaller one. We even did a mini meet-up at Hollywood Studios. Scott and I discussed it, and even though the Food and Wine Festival is extra fun that time of year, we really wanted to try the next gathering at the Magic Kingdom. After all, we are The "Main Street" Mouse, we needed to have a meet up actually near Main Street, U.S.A. The location was chosen, people were making arrangements to attend, and I was working on a little something extra for our staff. It was a stressful time, but in my head, I needed things to work, there were no exceptions. The hope and drive were there; I just had to pray for the best.

Disney World was crazy busy at this time, so for a bit there, we didn't go, but we kept busy regardless. My job isn't a 9-to-5 type of gig. It's morning until bedtime, believe it or not. Between the site, our new magazine, social media interaction, and posting, plus answering emails and questions from our followers, it's constant. Even on weekends. Among the frenzy, we do take time out for the kids and have family dinners and outings. The boys know that that mom is always in "work mode" most days, but sometimes I just have to stop. Sometimes I get burnt out, and I need a break. When I feel a break coming on, or feel myself getting bogged down, I'll do some scheduling of blogs and posts ahead of time, and walk away from the computer. I have to walk away. You can almost hear Elsa in your head shouting, "Enough!" but minus the throwing of ice everywhere. See, there's a Disney reference for everything if you try. We're all human, and we all have times where we need an extra hug or some words of encouragement.

The meet-up was coming, which was an expense, plus there was the expense of going home for my brother's wedding. I wasn't sure how we were going to do it all. A huge misconception people have at times is that a big following equals big money. Nothing could be further than the truth. The Main Street Mouse has almost 400,000 followers on Facebook, close to 30,000 on Instagram, plus other social media platforms. It's a great feeling; the sense of accomplishment is beyond words. But ... and there's a but ... what we do truly is a labor of love. We're not rich, by far. Doing this job is a struggle, but it's one I can't imagine not doing. Regrouping and recharging, that I can do. There are months that I honestly don't know how we get by, how we can put food on the table or pay our rent, but we find a way. Sure, we can't do expensive dinners, my kids can't go to the parks and pick out extra souvenirs or novelty items, but we are lucky in other ways. We live close to the parks, we have our health, we have a huge support system, and most importantly, we have each other. Every time things get hard, I have to remind myself that somewhere, someone else has it much worse than we do, and we need to be thankful for what we *do* have, rather than sad for what we don't. It's not always easy, but it can be accomplished with a little persistence.

That being said, we had staff coming to town before the meet-up. The night before the big group event, I wanted to do something for just them, something as a thank-you for all the help and support they give us. So, we started planning a house party for our staffers. We were going to invite them all to come to the house where we could cook for them, give them thank-you gifts, and have a relaxing time before the big day. I had a plan; I just needed to put it in motion.

CHAPTER TWENTY-EIGHT

Celebrate Good Times (on a Budget)

Since it was October, I started buying things here and there like Halloween plates and napkins, and ingredients to make cupcakes and snack foods. Instead of getting everything at once, I was gathering party goods as I saw them; it was cheaper. I wanted to get our staff some gifts, so I was spreading that out as well, buying things here and there. As an extra for their goody bags, I took our regular TMSM buttons and decorated them with ribbons and hot glue. Little things make a difference, especially when it's done from the heart. Saying thank-you is something my mom taught me from the time I could talk; I was pretty good about manners. Showing appreciation was also important to me, so I was doing whatever I could.

My friends Paula and Michelle were flying in for the meet-up again, on (I thought) Friday, the same night of the staff party. The night before, Scott told me we needed to run to Disney Springs to meet someone, and when we got there, the "someone" ended up being multiples: Paula and Michelle. Surprise! Lorraine went to pick them up from the airport a day early. They all had it planned and I had no clue. We walked into the Hangar Bar at Disney Springs, and there they were. Too often I put so much extra worry on myself, and it buries me. My plate was full, I didn't know how we'd get through, but having friends from home here with me was a relief. We stayed there for a bit, then came back to the house to catch up. The boys like to have a "dance party" when the aunties are here, so we played music, danced, and had fun until we were exhausted and went to bed. We had a big few days coming up, so we needed the rest.

Friday was the day of the staff party. We fussed all day to make sure the house was festively decorated, the gifts were in their bags, and the food was prepared. Before I knew it, my house was filled with people, and that was the first time since we moved that we had that many guests. It was the staffers and Main Streeters that we have had around for some time. Corey and his family, Autumn, the Michigan girls, our other writer Greg and his crew, Fran was in town from New York, and the "super fans" Janet and Cindy. It was so nice to have them there. After eating and visiting for a bit, I went in my room to get the gifts, and before passing them out I asked for everyone's attention. They know I'm sappy and sentimental, and they knew that tears were coming, but I wanted to thank them. I needed them to know how thankful I was for them, even on days where my job feels a little thankless.

So after all of that, I was standing in the kitchen doorway and Cindy came up and asked if I was okay. "I'm not sure," I told her. There was so much worry, so much work, so many ups and downs with running TMSM and now taking on an e-magazine, my emotions always take over and cause sleepless nights when they don't need to. I was concerned about the meet-up the next day, too, because as usual, I wanted to show our attendees a good time, as well as make sure they know they are appreciated. What happened next is something I won't ever forget. Cindy went over to Greg to talk, then came back and asked if I minded if we said a prayer, all of us. A prayer for strength, a prayer for the good that we were trying to do with TMSM, a prayer to ease heart and mind. Of course I said yes. Cindy began the prayer, and Greg finished it. A weight felt lifted, and it was one of the nicest things they could have done for us.

The next morning was meet-up time. There we were, once again, running around the house, trying to get ready, and trying to remember everything we needed, like buttons and prizes. It was going to be a long day. We headed out to the Magic Kingdom, running a bit behind and trying to get ourselves back toward the Haunted Mansion, as that was the first meeting spot of the day. Corey had texted Scott, saying there was already a crowd, and I thought he was kidding. One thing about Corey, he has such a dry sense of humor, he's hard to read at times. Is he serious, or is he just messing with us? We got near the spot, I walked around the corner, and soon realized Corey wasn't joking: there were probably 50 people there already. I asked

Autumn to give people name tags so I wouldn't forget names. These meet-up crowds were getting bigger and bigger, and I wanted to make sure I knew who was who. We took some pictures, then went on Haunted Mansion to start the day.

The group got bigger as the afternoon went on. Cast members at Pecos Bill were nice enough to give us a separate room for our large group to have lunch in. When we got to the Jungle Cruise, the skipper, Alex, knew who we were and was hoping to have the day off to attend our meet up. So he helped us out and got us boats for just our group so we could all ride together. The day was going perfect, thus far.

That evening, we chose a certain time to meet up in front of the castle for a big group photo. So many people were there, I was overwhelmed. I didn't want our group to clutter up the front of the castle for long. I asked our staffers to help me get the group together for the picture, but it wasn't happening too fast. Chuck took photos for Disney as his day job, but photography was also a favorite hobby. If anyone could get us organized for a picture with that many people in it, Chuck would be the guy. He and Scott wrangled and set up the crowd, and got us some great photos. Afterward, they took a picture, just the two of them, since they weren't in the group shot.

If I had to guess, we had almost 150 Main Streeters show up throughout the day. I couldn't have asked for more. The scheduled activities were done, but we still had people who wanted to hang around for more fun. Our group went to the Monsters, Inc Laugh Floor and almost filled the room with Main Streeters. When the "monster" chose someone from the crowd to interact with, he chose *me*. What are the chances? Our group was hooting and hollering, it was such a fun time. Before I knew it, Celebrate the Magic and Wishes were over, and the day was done. Out of all the meet-ups we have had, even now, that one was my favorite. Things couldn't have gone better. If not for TMSM, I wouldn't have met these wonderful people, and it gave me a renewed sense of purpose, to keep pushing and try harder.

CHAPTER TWENTY-NINE

Tis the Season

Like the year prior, Disney World wasted no time when it came to Christmas festivities. As soon as we got back to Florida, we began to figure out our work schedule and what events we needed to cover. It was announced that the first lighting of Cinderella Castle was coming, as was the kick-off of the Osborne Lights. Sadly, with all the changes happening over at Hollywood Studios, the Osborne Lights were going to be a casualty, and this was their last year. There was also information for the ABC Christmas Parade taping, so we had to make time for that, too. The weather was much hotter than the year before. I wore a jacket to the parade taping in 2014, and in 2015 I was wearing a tank top and sweating to death. The director of the parade kept telling people to not look hot when he yelled action. How do you do that? The year before it was, "Pretend it's not raining." It's fascinating to see how they put these productions together. Now with the magazine, we have to make sure we have extra pictures and content written, so the works seems to never stop. Busy times, all the time. The day of the concert taping, though, one of the performers was very late, and people were standing almost three hours in the heat waiting. We didn't want to lose our spot. Producer David Foster came out, and got everyone water bottles to help them stay hydrated. Parade MC Mark Daniel kept asking if people were feeling okay. It was really something to be there. Christmas taping, fighting heat exhaustion. That's Florida for you.

Before going home to Michigan for Christmas, we decided to do a small meet-up at the Osborne Lights, since it was ending soon. Well, unlucky for us, we weren't the only people wanting to get some final memories out of the lights. By noon that day they closed the parking lot at Hollywood Studios. Cast members were re-routing people to

Epcot to park, then get bussed over. That's what we had to do; it was beyond busy. By the time we got to the park, we heard that Animal Kingdom was the parking lot they were using to bus people from,

The area by the lights was wall-to-wall people, and I wasn't sure if people would find us, or if they'd even show up due to the parking nightmare. A lot of people had to cancel, but we did have some Main Streeters there, so it worked out alright. There was something about the Osborne Spectacle of Dancing Lights that really tugged on the heartstrings. So many were sad it was being retired, myself included.

In other news, times were changing across the world, and it was getting worse. We had witnessed a terror attack in Paris, then in California. I was nervous to turn the television on, as I didn't want the boys to see the tragedies and worry for our safety. Disney guests were starting to worry, too. My inbox was getting flooded with messages from readers asking if Disney was increasing security, and if it was safe to come here. My friend and new staffer Susanne was at the Magic Kingdom with her family one morning and she sent me a message with photos. Disney was putting in metal detectors at the front of the park. Security was tighter, and sadly in these times, it had to be. Universal Studios had put in metal detectors as well, but every guest had to walk through. Disney was doing a random selection, so most guests were not checked. We went to the park to watch fireworks shortly after, and instead of cast members directing parade crowds on Main Street, it was Orange County sheriffs.

Shortly after that, it was time for our long drive north. Granted, we were just home at Halloween, but I was looking forward to being with family for the holidays. It was once again time to dig out our winter coats, hats, gloves, and boots, and pack them up. We only use them for about two weeks out of the year now, which was still funny to me. We got home, did our annual trip to Bronners Christmas Wonderland, and took the parents to see the new Star Wars movie, *The Force Awakens*.

Work still has to be done, even though we're not in Florida. Truthfully, I'm glad we're not in Florida at Christmas time. Disney parks are so packed that it's miserable; sometimes the parks hit capacity and they have to turn people away. That's not fun. The only crowds we have in Michigan are at the after-Christmas sale at Kohls. So, between shopping and visiting, we still have to work. What's funny ... well, not funny, but strange: no one in my extended family ever asks me about my job. No one. My parents ask, my friends ask, my sister in law asks, but that's it. I'm not sure why. Is it hurtful? Yes. I try not to let it bother me, we just keep on keeping on, and do our best.It takes a certain type of person to be your own motivation, regardless of what's happening. Scott and I push each other to keep going, and we were doing a decent job of it.

Christmas Eve was at my parents' house, which is our preferred place to have it. They have the party house. Lots of places to sit, my dad built a bar for the basement, plus if the kids get tired they can go to bed if people stay late. We stayed all the way until the end of the year, so we could welcome 2016 with our family and friends. Then it was time to go. Little did I know that the upcoming year would be one of the most challenging of my life, but I was grateful that 2015 was a pretty fun and adventurous year overall, with more good points than bad.

CHAPTER THIRTY

Ups and Downs

The new year was here, and I felt like a jumbled-up mess. The Main Street Mouse was going okay, but I felt a little restless. Our business is so competitive, and I felt we needed to step it up. There were suggestions of doing more videos for our YouTube channel, so that was on the list. Facebook was also just beginning to explore live feeds and I knew there were possibilities there. You have to change things around sometimes and keep up with the times or you can fall behind. Change is hard in that respect, too. I don't like to do things too differently all the time, even when I have to. But, it's the nature of the job.

More changes were coming. We had gotten some new volunteers for the magazine in 2015, and they were leaving us to focus on a new project. I was thankful for the help, but knew that again, we'd have to figure things out and work that much harder. *The Main Street Monthly* wasn't doing what I hoped it would do; it's hard to get your product out there. When we first started this journey years ago, Facebook didn't put restrictions on pages the way they do now. If you want your posts seen, you basically have to pay Facebook to show them to your audience, and that never used to be the case. We prided ourselves on never having to pay for our following; we built everything organically, and I couldn't afford to throw money into Facebook even if I wanted to. Other pages were feeling the same pinch, so it wasn't just us. All we could do was keep plugging away, and keep working hard.

The year was pressing on. We did another birthday for me at the Magic Kingdom, but we ate breakfast at 'Ohana at the Polynesian Resort this time. Money was tight, so that was pretty much my present, and that was fine. Also coming back around was Epcot's Flower and Garden Festival. I couldn't believe how fast time was flying. Writing for the site was easy, but with the magazine, we were doing double duty when it came to photos and content. Susanne was on the staff full time now, and also volunteered for the magazine, which was a huge help. Our staff was small, but we still managed to get things done.

Word got around that more permanent closures were coming over at Hollywood Studios, so we were going to plan a meet-up for that, or at least try. Easter was early, so in an effort to stay busy, we spent the day at the Magic Kingdom, and saw the Happy Easter Parade. Among all of this, we learned that our friend Corey's father passed away. Corey got a lot of his love for Disney through his father, and we were heartbroken for him. He and his wife and kids had become like family to us; they were part of our TMSM family, and when one of us hurts, we all do. We dedicated that month's issue to Corey's father, Harold. It was a small gesture, but we needed to do something. What just happened in their family brought a lot of my own fears to the surface. Being away from family, there is always that worry that someone you love could get hurt or sick, and we wouldn't be there for them.

The first weekend in April was busy. There was a convention in town called Spooky Empire, and we were invited to come check it out and do a write up for our Off TMSM section. At this point, we actually closed the other two sites, Off TMSM and TMSM Geek, and decided to keep everything under the main platform, TMSM. We still did write ups and such for other things to do around town, but felt separate sites were just extra work and not necessary.

Spooky Empire is a pop-culture type of convention, much like a comic con, but with the addition of scary movies and other fan favorites. I never thought I'd be someone who loves these types of conventions, but my husband converted me; they really are a lot of fun. Andrew and Aidan love it, too. That night, we met some actors from *Nightmare on Elm Street*, met someone from the television show *Ghost Hunters* while standing in line for the ATM, and my favorite part, I got to meet Anthony Michael Hall. I'm an 80s movie buff, and I had seen *Sixteen Candles* and *The Breakfast Club* so much that I knew the lines from the movies. He was really nice, too, took some pics with us, and signed a poster. My inner 80s child was thrilled.

The next day was when the closures were happening over at Hollywood Studios. It was the last day for Lights, Motors, Action! Extreme Stunt Show, Monster's Inc Meet & Greet, Honey I Shrunk the Kids Playground, Watto's Grotto, and the entire Streets of America area, where those beloved Osborne Lights used to shine. We met some friends there, and were lucky enough to catch the very last performance of the stunt show. The drivers and crew put their all into that last run, and got a standing ovation once it was over.

Afterward, we walked over to the Honey I Shrunk the Kids area for one final walkthrough, and they were already getting ready to close. Monsters Inc had also wrapped up, so we just walked through the Streets of America and took some photos for the last time. There goes that whole "change is hard" emotion again. Disney always has things in the works, so the hope was that whatever is coming next will be bigger and better.

More busy times were coming, as my parents were coming to town for their spring visit. Not only my parents, but my brother and sister-in-law were coming, too. They rented a house right around the corner from where we live, so they'd be close by. Neither Greg nor Amee had been to Disney since they were little kids, and didn't remember much about the experience. For me, that's a green light to throw some Disney magic their way. My brother isn't and had never been a Disney kid. When we were younger, he had other interests, and Disney wasn't on the top of his list like it was mine. Actually, his last trip was that same trip that made my dad get a bad taste in his mouth about Disney. I had my work cut out for me.

Their visit here was great. One day I went with just my mom and Amee to Disney Springs for lunch. We did one Disney park day—the Magic Kingdom, of course. It was also my mother's birthday. My hope was that they all would have fun day ... and they did. I knew Amee would be fine, she has fun anyplace she goes. Greg, on the other hand, was going to be a harder sell, or so I thought. To my surprise, he had a fun day, too. We all went on rides, got snacks, and took lots of pictures, and by the time we left, I actually got a picture of Greg and Amee wearing Mickey ears. Success!

The visit we had was so good it pained me that they were leaving. Having them staying right around the corner was wonderful, and I wished they actually lived there. Saying goodbye is the hardest part, and I was really feeling it that time. We had been so busy that it was nice to take a break for company coming to town, but that was coming to a close and we needed to get back to the grind.

CHAPTER THIRTY-ONE

Expect the Unexpected

The live feeds were going pretty well for the site, our members were really enjoying it, and on my end, I loved being able to share the parks with them in real time. The new Town Center at Disney Springs was getting ready to open soon, so our readers were excited for that and wanted to know the details on all that was coming. In the meantime, I was having some health issues that were keeping me a bit down. Duty calls, no matter how bad you feel, and I was trying to keep the site running up to speed, regardless of what was happening with me. I had been so busy with work and my family's visit that I hadn't had time to think, or realize that things weren't right with me, or possibly why. My stomach was sour and I was feeling really tired. Even though I was told years before that I was done having children due to medical reasons, we found out that I was pregnant. Talk about a shock. I didn't know what we were going to do, or how we were going to handle something that we weren't prepared for, but we felt blessed. How would we afford this? Do we tell people or do we wait? All these things were running through my head, and I wasn't sure what to do. I called my parents to tell them. They were surprised but really happy to be getting a new grandchild. We'd make it work somehow, but in the meantime, we would keep in quiet. Telling the boys was scary because I wasn't sure how they'd react, but they did fine. Well, Andrew did fine, Aidan cried, as he's the "baby" in the house besides Jack, our dog.

The new Sprinkles Cupcakes was getting ready to open, and we were invited to the media event to try it out. I wasn't feeling well, but we still went. I knew I wasn't going to be able to hide our newest surprise for long, so I just wore a loose dress.

Not long after that, our friend Fran and her husband were coming to town for a visit, and I knew that if I saw her, she'd know what was going on. Scott and I knew we could trust her to keep our secret. Her reaction was just what we needed to hear; she was thrilled. I was so sick that it was hard to feel upbeat and excited, but I knew the sickness was temporary, and we needed to keep working.

The rest of the Town Center area opened and we spent more time at Disney Springs to get details for the site and magazine. The feedback we got from readers was mixed. Some loved it, and thought it was a great addition to the area; others, not so much. They felt that it didn't go with the rest of Disney Springs, and felt more like a strip mall. TMSM is just the messenger, so we only report on what we see, but let them vent, regardless.

In addition to working and keeping up with all the changes that were happening at Disney, we were having to go to doctor visits. Costly doctor visits. I thought we barely made ends meet before, but now with prenatal visits, well, it was rough. Things were going alright, my belly was growing, and we were getting used to having another Disney prince or princess in the house.

Then, at one of our appointments, we learned that something may be wrong with the baby. The staff at the doctor's office was less than impressive or helpful; they basically sent me home to wait. The waiting was agony. They kept charging us for tests and visits, but gave us no answers. How could this be happening? Scott and I were trying our best to be positive and go through daily life like all was fine, but we were scared. Keeping my fear contained was important because I didn't want the boys to suspect something was wrong. They were excited at the idea of having a baby sister or brother, and I didn't want to worry them.

Corey and his family came to town for the Flower and Garden Festival at Epcot, and we met them. Obviously, they knew what was going on, too. While we were at the festival, I got an upsetting message from Chuck's son, Chris. None of us knew, as they kept it quiet, but Chuck was very sick, and things weren't looking good. This bit of news shook our Disney Ohana, and we felt helpless. Chuck was such a big part of the site and the meet-ups, and a huge supporter. All we could do was wait.

That same weekend I had some blood work done, and we were like sitting ducks waiting on the results. More waiting. That Wednesday I was feeling pretty tired, but it was Aidan's birthday, and for his sake, I was going to do my best to give him a good day. He wanted to go to the mall and spend his birthday money, then go to Cracker Barrel for dinner. Seemed easy enough. At bedtime I was feeling even worse, but I thought if I just went to sleep, I would feel better in the morning. I'm sad to say, that wasn't the case. Our world was shattered that next morning, as we lost the baby at home. No call from the doctor, no warning, no test results ... nothing. Until this happened to me, I never fully understood the complete and utter devastation that losing a pregnancy would cause, and now it was staring me in the face.

When I started TMSM, I made a deal with God. I told Him if he gave me a platform, that I promised to do good in the world with it. We brought together a lot of people, put out positive information, honored people with our acts of kindness blogs, allowed people to post and ask for prayers and "pixie dust" when they needed it, and do so without judgement. I thought this baby was something good coming back to us, as silly as that sounds. I guess that's not how it works, though. That's not a rational way to think, I know that now, but at the time I was angry. We were broken, mentally, physically, spiritually ... just at a complete and total loss. Why would we go through the financial strain, the sickness, the fear, and eventually the acceptance ... only to have it ripped away? No answers were coming. Telling my boys was awful; seeing them cry was even worse. Having to tell my parents was awful, too. That same week my mom made a little memory garden in her yard for the baby. It was her way to cope.

Me? I wasn't coping, I wasn't doing anything. I barely left my bedroom for weeks, only when I had to. I knew I had the site to take care of, the magazine was coming due on June 1, and I had nothing to offer. The new summer activities were beginning at Animal Kingdom, and I couldn't go. I was on bed rest. How could this be happening? Eventually, I had no choice but to get up and pull myself together, as more bad news had come. We got the word that Chuck had passed away. Another heartbreak. We were all at such a loss. Chuck had left a huge imprint on our hearts, and he was going to be sorely missed. So much sadness, in such a short time. But why? No answers were coming, only heartache and confusion.

CHAPTER THIRTY-TWO

Finding Strength

When tragic things happen, it's an eye opener, for a couple of reasons. First, you really get put to the test, and you figure out how strong you actually are and what you can fully bear. Just like when we moved, I kept saying I didn't think I could do it, that I wasn't strong, that I wasn't brave. In this case, I never thought I could withstand something like this, but when you have no other choice but to go on, that's exactly what you do. Second, you discover who is really there for you when you are completely down for the count. The number is far fewer than one would think, and that part was very sad. I know that the loss of a baby is an uncomfortable subject, no one really "knows" what to say. Sometimes, all you want is for someone to say "I'm sorry" or "I love you." That's it. Those words can make a huge difference when you are feeling empty inside. I'm still struggling with that part. Family should care. People you thought were friends should care. Sometimes you have to forgive, not for them, but for yourself. It's hard. A lot of friends did step up, however, and were a great comfort. I'm thankful. I was glad that we never made an announcement on TMSM with baby Mickey ears or anything like that, as we had planned to do. It would have been worse to have to tell the world that our newest blessing wasn't meant to be. The only reason I chose to talk about this here is that it really is part of our story, and because many women feel shame when it comes to miscarriage. I'm hoping by speaking out it will encourage and comfort others who have been through it as well, and make them realize that they're not alone and not at fault.

In addition to our own grieving, we were also feeling horrible about Chuck. And his son. The service for Chuck wasn't going to be for two weeks, and I was still recovering, but I knew I was going to go.

I wanted to be able to help somehow, too. They were raising money for his funeral expenses, so I wrote about him and shared the link to his fundraiser on the site. It wasn't much, but Scott and I both wanted to help. The day of Chuck's service finally came, and we did indeed attend. Cindy was there, too; we sat together. During the service, the pastor asked for people to share stories about Chuck, and I did have the courage to speak up. Some of Chuck's other children were there, and I thought it might be a good thing to share with them how special their father was to us and our Disney family. I told the story that I wrote about earlier, how Chuck reminded me that I had family in Florida that first Christmas we were here. He gave me words of comfort when I needed them, and I'd always be grateful.

Life is funny sometimes. Things can change in the blink of an eye, and nothing can be taken for granted. Every day is a gift, people are a blessing, and when bad things happen, we get those reminders front and center. It's hard, but we have to do our best to move forward. I'm still trying.

It felt like summer was off to the worst start ever. Andrew's birthday came, and I got myself out of bed for that, too, to take him shopping and to dinner. My body was still very sore, and I tired quickly, but I wanted to give him a good day. We had all been through so much, and I wanted to give the boys some reprieve, to try to give them a sense of normal again. Andrew had a good day, so I was happy.

Shortly after that, the tragedy at the Pulse night club happened, and this whole area was in mourning. Then there was the incident with the little boy at the Grand Floridian. I was having to report on things that were unbearable to think about, but it's part of the job. When things happen that are hard, I try to inform our readers in the most delicate way possible. You never know who is reading what you write; it could be someone who is personally effected by what's happening, so using tact and compassion is important. I was feeling a bit lost as to what direction to take to make things better. The best thing for me was to get back to work as soon as I could.

There was more at Disney that we needed to cover, and I had to get with it. Hollywood Studios was debuting their new fireworks and laser show, Star Wars; A Galactic Spectacular. We went early, as we usually do when something is making its debut, staked out our spot, and recorded the new show. It was indeed spectacular; they chose their title well. A lot of the blogging community and media was there, of course, but we held our own. I had gotten to the point that their opinions didn't matter. We had been through so much, and coming out stronger on the other side was my best option.

One of our sponsors was there, too. We had talked a bit, I was trying to explain why I had been laying low the past few weeks, and I finally just told her why. The understanding and compassion I got was very much appreciated. Sometimes that's all you need, an ear to bend.

The following night, there was a candlelight vigil at the Magic Kingdom for the victims of the Pulse shooting. Talk about a hard thing to cover. But it was important to come together and show respect. Some of our readers were planning on attending as well, so we chose a meet-up spot so we could all stand near each other. Our photographer friend Joe was in town with his wife, they were there, too. There's safety and solidarity in numbers, and I was glad to have them there. I felt it would be disrespectful to do any live feeds of the memorial; that's not what it was about. It was about remembering those who were tragically lost, and it's not something to capitalize on. Disney handled it well. They gave out pins to those who attended. Such a sad reason to be there, and my heart goes out to all of those who lost a loved one. We wrote about it after the fact, because people were curious, but we handled it the best way we could.

CHAPTER THIRTY-THREE

Living the Dream the Best We Can

Disney had been full of news that summer, and it was our job to stay on top of it all. Another story to cover was the opening of the new Frozen Ever After ride, the one that replaced Maelstrom in Norway at Epcot. The line for the ride was crazy that morning; roughly a 5-hour wait. We had a FastPass so we were able to get on and get photos and video for our readers. It was the first day in a long time that I felt somewhat like my old self, and really enjoyed being back in reporter mode. So many people on the site were waiting to hear what Frozen Ever After was all about, and I was happy to get that info for them. Soarin' had just re-opened after a 6-month closure for refurbishment, so we went and got footage of that, too. Back to business … and we were doing okay.

While I was down, Andrew really stepped up and helped get photos for the magazine. I was really proud of him. He kept the interest up and started contributing to the magazine, and joined the photography club at school. It's a great hobby for him.

In addition to that, we were coming up on our one-year anniversary of the magazine, and putting the finishing touches on the anniversary issue. It was hard to believe that a year went by. I remember that first issue, and how scared we were to launch something new. That's the fear when you have your own business. Things are always hit or miss, feast or famine. We're never sure what people will respond to, but we keep trying. That being said, we had to go to the Magic Kingdom to get last minute photos for the July issue, as we were also getting ready to go home for a summer visit once the magazine was done. We really needed some family time, so we let the kids choose what they wanted to do, and they chose Splash Mountain. They got good and soaked ... and were thrilled.

The week before "vacation" I had been to three of the four Disney World parks, getting content for the site and magazine. In our ventures out, I got to meet some of our readers, which I loved. There are days when I wonder if we do a good-enough job, or if the hours we put into TMSM make a difference. When I have people come up to us in the parks, it reaffirms my belief in the site and it does my heart good. At Hollywood Studios, one family spotted us and came up to say hello. We ended up watching the fireworks with them and chatted for quite awhile. To me, that's the best. Meeting the people who support us is a gift. It helps keep us motivated and focused, and we thank them for that.

The summer went along pretty decently. We passed our first anniversary for the magazine, and got some excellent new volunteers to help us. Vacation to Michigan was once again needed, especially after everything that we had been through. Some friends here wondering if we'd come back to Florida after that, and I can understand why they'd feel that way. But we did come back, and we were raring to go. Maybe that's where strength comes in. Strength that you didn't even realize that you had. School was starting earlier than usual, so we were trying to make the most of what was left of the summer. On the work front, we had a festival upcoming and I was asked to be a media guest, and of course our annual meet-up was also on the horizon. One unexpected surprise? The chance to write this book, and that's where I'd like to wrap up.

When I was asked to write my story, I not only was excited, but felt like there needed to be an extra purpose that went with it. Like with all we do at The Main Street Mouse and its spinoffs, there is meaning behind it, and the goal to bring happiness and to inspire. The note I wrote to our readers on our one-year Florida anniversary says so much. It's something that I still mean, maybe even more so. In life we don't get many opportunities to take chances or live out a dream. Those are the times when we need to stop waiting for an opportunity to come, and just decide to make one for ourselves. I had talked for years and years about moving to Florida, but it was just talk. Also, I was a huge Disney fan my entire life and wanted to do something Disney related, but that was talk, too. Life is so full of ups and downs, and I was at the point that it was either now or never, time to stop dreaming and start doing. I never thought of myself as brave, or a risk taker, or strong ... not ever. Even when we decided to move south, I still didn't. It's like a cold swimming pool. Either you dip your toe in the water and get in slowly, or you just hold your breath and jump. That's what I did, I jumped. To this day, I don't know how I did it.

I do know that if I can chase my dream and face my fears, anyone can. It doesn't have to be the same for you; not everyone wants to move away from home, or have a Disney business. You can learn from me, though, whatever your dream is, whether it's changing jobs, or learning a new skill, or finding a way to make a difference in your community. Don't be afraid, just hold your breath and jump. I'm so glad that I did.

No matter what happens from here on out, I know a few things for sure. We took risks. We had people who believed in us whole-heartedly. We went through some horrible things and came out stronger on the other side. No matter what happened, we kept moving forward, just like Walt said a long time ago. Never let anyone tell you that you can't do something, because indeed you can. If you don't have someone to be a champion or cheerleader for you, be your own. Naysayers don't matter, find your inner strength, be brave. I did. Just like the line in the movie *Tangled*: "Go, live your dream."

A SAD ADDENDUM

Since the completion of this book, we lost one of our biggest supporters, Fran Randazzo Hesse. Fran was my most vocal cheerleader, always believing in me and pushing me to do more. I will always be thankful for her support, love, and friendship.

About the Author

Michele Atwood is a lifelong Disney fan and the co-owner and lead writer of the popular Disney fan site The Main Street Mouse and its spinoff e-magazine, *The Main Street Monthly*. Michele's writing has been featured across various media platforms since the creation of The Main Street Mouse back in 2010. She and her family are originally from southeast Michigan, but relocated to the Orlando area.

More Books from Theme Park Press

Theme Park Press is the largest independent publisher of Disney, Disney-related, and general interest theme park books in the world, with over 100 new releases each year.

We're always looking for new talent.

For a complete catalog, including book descriptions and excerpts, please visit:

ThemeParkPress.com

themeparkpress.com/books/haunted-mansion.htm

Welcome, Foolish Readers!

Join your new Ghost Host, Jeff Baham, as he recounts the colorful, chilling history of the Haunted Mansion and pulls back the shroud on its darkest secrets in this definitive book about Disney's most ghoulish attraction. With exclusive photos and Imagineer commentary; updated for 2017.

Lions and Tigers and Cast Members

Armed with a freshly minted degree in anthropology, Arielle Tuan found her job prospects less than hoped for. Then she heard of the professional internships at Disney's Animal Kingdom for college graduates interested in conservation. Apply? Why not! And from there her adventure begins....

themeparkpress.com/books/arielle-animal-kingdom.htm

The Imagineering Graveyard

On an alternate earth, Walt Disney World guests are taking in the thrills of Thunder Mesa, braving the Beastly Kingdom, marveling at Villains Mountain, and staying the night at Disney's Persian Resort. Want to join them? This is your guidebook to the theme park that Disney never built.

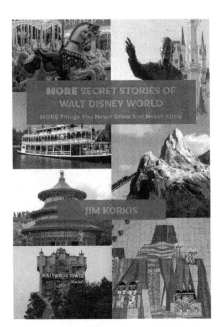

Oh, You Didn't Know?

Just when you think you *do* know everything there is to know about Walt Disney World, here comes Jim Korkis with a new book full of stuff you won't easily find anywhere else. From the theme parks and resorts to "beyond the berm", this is the Disney that Disney forgot.

Sensible Touring Plans

What do those Walt Disney World guidebook authors know? Well, they know a lot, and sometimes that's the problem: they forget what it's like to visit Disney World with a family, not as a ruthless ride maximizer. *This* guidebook shelves the statistics and preaches the practical.

themeparkpress.com/books/not-so-evil-stepmother.htm

A Monkey Paw in the Magic Kingdom

When R.J. and Suzanne Ogren 'remember the magic' of Walt Disney World, they're not remembering their trips to the most magical place on earth, they're remembering their jobs: Suzanne as a character performer, R.J. as an artist. Their backstage stories are like none you've ever read before.

themeparkpress.com/books/remembering-magic.htm

Made in the USA
Lexington, KY
10 April 2017